# Quiet Places of the Heart

## in Winter

# Contents

# Contents

*No matter how many times I've experienced the soft intrusion of the
first snowfall of the season, I'm always enchanted by its coming.*

DEBRA KLINGSPORN
*Soul Searching*

Yellow leaves lay rustling
on the ground, bleak winds
went whistling through the
naked trees, and cold,
white Winter snow
fell softly down.

**LOUISA MAY
ALCOTT**

*"Little Annie's
Dream"*

# The Holiness of Winter

❄

*The LORD shall preserve your going out and your coming
in from this time forth, and even forevermore.*

PSALM 121:8

I t's hard to think of cold and sleet glorifying God.
Winter seems to most of us a dead time, a
season when nothing is happening. We
scarcely want to poke our noses outside the
house, and when we do, we find only "the
bleak midwinter," a wearying emptiness.
The world and its creatures, including
ourselves, seem to long for the enlivening
touch of spring to resurrect them from the
dead of winter. . . .

[Yet] what seems like death to us is only
sleep. The world, spent with a summer's
work to make an autumn's bounty, is taking
its necessary rest.

In this sleep of winter, as in our own sleep, life renews itself. The
hurry of doing and making is replaced by peaceful rest. Winter's peace
also brings with it
conditions and qualities
congenial to the spiritual
life. There is *stillness.* If we
pay attention there are new
ways of seeing the familiar, revealing new aspects of things we
thought we knew. For those who seek it, there is *solitude.*

*Week 1*

*The wintry portions of my life
are those which often give birth
to a deeper understanding of who
you created me to be O God.*

PENNY TRESSLER

❄

## DAVID RENSBERGER
*The Holiness of Winter*

The year has slipped across the crest and is rolling head-long down the winter side. Today I had to build fires in the stove and fireplace and nurse them home to comfort. The damp woods are wonderful with the scent of cedar smoke in the air.

GLORIA
GAITHER

We Have this Moment

# Living from the Center Outward

❄

*You will show me the path of life;*
*in Your presence is fullness of joy.*

PSALM 16:11

Living with purpose does not eliminate spontaneity or the relaxation of lingering over a cup of coffee. A purposeful life in not lived at such a frenzied pitch that every hour is like a hamster's jaw that we cram full with as much as we can. Furthermore, living a purposeful life is not like writing a script God is some— how obligated to follow, as though my fine but fleshly efforts could guarantee the realized goal. God has His own ways of keeping us flexible and dependent on Him in our planning. After all, "The mind of man plans his way, but the LORD directs his steps." (Proverbs 16:9)

*When I can do nothing else,*
*it is enough to have picked up*
*a straw for the love of God.*

BROTHER
LAWRENCE

❄

To live purposefully is to live as Jesus lived, with a clear sense of direction and calling. He extricated Himself from the clinging multitudes who would have gladly made Him a cult personality. Even His closest friends could not deter Him from His mission. He lived from the center outward. His eyes were riveted toward the Cross.

STACY AND PAULA RINEHART
*Living in Light of Eternity*

# Acts of Compassion

❄

*The work of righteousness will be peace, and the effect
of righteousness, quietness and assurance forever.*

ISAIAH 32:17

One day last summer, hiking with two of the children through the hills of north Georgia, I came to a tiny cabin clinging to a rocky ledge. Behind a picket fence a white-haired mountain woman was working in her garden. When we stopped to admire her flowers, she told us that she lived there all alone. My city-bred youngsters regarded her with wonder. "How," asked one, "do you keep from being lonesome?" "Oh," she said, "if that feeling starts to come on in the summertime, I take a bunch of flowers to some shut-in. And if it's winter, I just go out and feed the birds!" An act of compassion—that was her instinctive antidote for loneliness. And it made her immune.

ARTHUR GORDON
*A Touch of Wonder*

# The Bread of Life

❄

*Blessed shall be your basket and your kneading bowl.*

DEUTERONOMY 28:5

Nothing says "home" more appealingly than the earthy frankincense of bread fresh from the oven. A peasant comes home from the field and the promise reaches out through the open door. A stockbroker returns in the evening to his high-rise condo and finds it transformed by the same miracle of basic domesticity. . . . The aroma of bread triggers a mood of shelter and sanctuary. . . .

*We don't get a bowlful of strength or grace to put on a shelf and reach for in time of need. It is given us on the spot.*

EDITH SCHAEFFER

The wonder of food is beautifully expressed in the Hebrew meal *berakoth* [blessing]: "Blessed art thou, Yahweh, our God, King of the Universe, who bringest forth bread from the earth." This table prayer was used in the years that Christ walked upon our planet. It is probably the blessing that he himself offered on a regular basis.

With redeemed imaginations, we can almost hear him speak the words. . . . Because bread is bread from one generation to another, we can almost get a whiff of the very loaves he blessed.

GREGORY POST &
CHARLES TURNER
*The Feast*

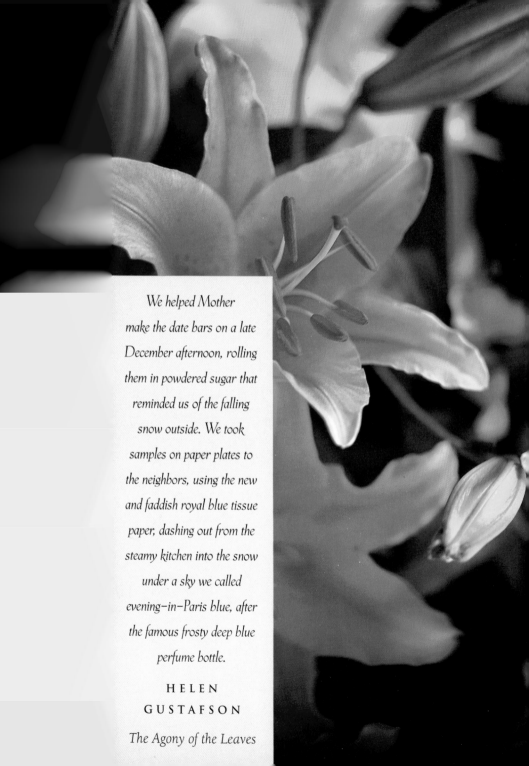

We helped Mother
make the date bars on a late
December afternoon, rolling
them in powdered sugar that
reminded us of the falling
snow outside. We took
samples on paper plates to
the neighbors, using the new
and faddish royal blue tissue
paper, dashing out from the
steamy kitchen into the snow
under a sky we called
evening–in–Paris blue, after
the famous frosty deep blue
perfume bottle.

HELEN
GUSTAFSON

*The Agony of the Leaves*

# The Freedom of Selflessness

❄

*The LORD is your keeper; the LORD is
your shade at your right hand.*

PSALM 121:5

We are conditioned nowadays . . . to define everything as a problem. A little girl on a TV commercial pipes, "I have this terrible *problem* with my hair! But my mommy bought No More Tangles, and now there's no more tangles!". . .

Life is full of things we can't do anything about, but which we are supposed to do something with. "He himself endured a cross and thought nothing of its shame because of the joy." A very different story from the one which would have been written if Jesus had been prompted by the spirit of our own age: "Don't just endure the cross—*think* about it, talk about it, share it, express your gut-level feelings, get in touch with yourself, find out who you are, define the problem, analyze it, get counseling, get the experts' opinions, discuss solutions, work through it." Jesus endured. He thought *nothing* of the shame. The freedom, the freshness of that valiant selflessness is like a strong wind. How badly such a wind is needed to sweep away the pollution of our self-preoccupation!

*When God develops character,
He works on it throughout
a lifetime . . . He's
never in a hurry.*

CHARLES
SWINDOLL

ELISABETH ELLIOT
*Love Has a Price Tag*

# Notes

❄

# Stop the Tide

❄

> LORD, You will establish peace for us,
> for You have also done all our works in us.

ISAIAH 26:12

Have you ever stood ankle-deep in the ocean? Gradually, wave upon wave washes about your feet, rearranging and depositing sand. And if you stand there long enough, you will find not only your feet, but your legs also buried beneath the sand. You don't have to do anything. It is enough to do nothing.

It is the same in the Christian life. You don't have to do anything to sink into worldly patterns of thinking and living. The world system in which we live floods in, wave upon wave. . . .

Our everyday environment seduces, taunts, and rages against the Christ-life within us. Without concentrated, deliberate action on our part to nourish our spiritual life, the oncoming tide wears away the undergirding foundation of our faith. To stanch the flow, to control the erosion, Christians must do more than hold our skirts higher. We must spend time apart with God. There is no growth in holiness apart from it.

*God's glory is
not only love. It is
also holiness.*

JOHN MURRAY

### JEAN FLEMING
*Finding Focus in a Whirlwind World*

*You have set all the borders*
*of the earth; You have made*
*summer and winter.*

PSALM 74:17

## *Broken Toys*

*The joy of the LORD is your strength.*

NEHEMIAH 8:10

Waiting certainly plays an enormous role in the unfolding story of God's relationship to man. It is God's oft-repeated way of teaching us that His power is real and that He can answer our prayers without interference and manipulation from us.

But we have such trouble getting *our* will, *our* time schedules out of the way. Much of the time we act like a child who brings a broken toy to his father to be mended. The father gladly takes the toy and begins work. Then after a while, childlike impatience takes over. Why is it taking so long?. . .

Finally in desperation, he snatches the toy from the father's hands and walks off with it, saying rather bitterly that he hadn't really thought his father could fix it anyway. . . .

On the other hand, whenever we are trustful enough to leave our "broken toy" with the Father, not only do we eventually get it back gloriously restored, but are also handed a surprising plus. We find . . . that during the dark waiting period when self-effort had ceased, a spurt of astonishing spiritual growth took place in us.

*Prayer is a means God uses to give us what He wants.*

W. BINGHAM HUNTER

# Week 2

CATHERINE MARSHALL

*Adventures in Prayer*

*When I was a child, winters were long and cold. And I loved it. I liked feeling the clouds of snowflakes on my face, I liked sledding and, in my own way, skating across ponds or even puddles of ice.... I charged through neighbors' yards knee–high with snow, prospecting for snowmen, the best ones, of course, with carrot noses.*

CAROL
DECHELLIS
HILL

*"Icicles"*

# The Gift of Faith

❄

*Let the hearts of those rejoice who seek the LORD.*

PSALM 105:3

Faith is a gift of God. Without it there would be no life. Our work, to bear fruit, to belong only to God, to be deserving, must be built on faith. Christ said: "I was hungry, I was naked, I was sick, I was homeless, and you did that for me." All our work is based on faith in these words.

If faith is lacking, it is because there is too much selfishness, too much concern for personal gain. For faith to be true, it has to be generous and loving. Love and faith go together; they complete each other. . . .

An Australian came the other day to make a large donation. But after making the donation he said: "This is something outside of myself; now I want to give something of myself." Since then, he comes regularly to the Home for the Dying to shave the sick and talk with them. He gives not only his money but also his time. He could have spent both his money and time on himself, but he wanted to spend himself instead.

*Giving ourselves is the most costly gift, and the most valuable.*

JANETTE OKE

MOTHER TERESA
*The Love of Christ*

# The Flow of God's Love

*Blessed are those who hunger and thirst
for righteousness, for they shall be filled.*

MATTHEW 5:6

I love a story I once heard about Leonardo da Vinci. According to the legend, some lads were visiting the famous artist. One of them knocked over a stack of canvases. This upset the artist because he was working very quietly and sensitively. He became angry, threw his brush, and hurled some harsh words to the hapless little fellow, who ran crying from the studio.

The artist was now alone again, and he tried to continue his work. He was trying to paint the face of Jesus, but he couldn't do it. His creativity had stopped.

Leonardo da Vinci put down his brush. He went out and walked the streets and the alleys until he found the little boy. He said, "I'm sorry, son; I shouldn't have spoken so harshly. . . . "

He took the boy back into the studio with him. They smiled as the face of Jesus came quite naturally from the master's brush. That face has been an inspiration to millions ever since.

ROBERT SCHULLER
*The Be Happy Attitudes*

# *Chosen by God*

❄

*O LORD, You are the portion of my inheritance
and my cup; You maintain my lot.*

PSALM 16:5

The year 1809 was a very good year. Of course those who were alive that year didn't know that. Only history tells the story. Those who were living in 1809 were focused on Napoleon. . . .

During that same period of time, thousands of babies were born in Britain and in America. But who cared about babies and bottles and cribs and cradles while Napoleon was doing his thing in Austria.

*O God, give me a
heart frameable to
Thy will.*

PURITAN PRAYER

❄

Well, someone should have cared, because in 1809 William Gladstone was born in Liverpool. Alfred Tennyson began his life in Lincolnshire. Oliver Wendell Holmes cried out for the first time in Cambridge, Massachusetts. A few miles away in Boston, Edgar Allan Poe began his brief and tragic sojourn on earth. That same year, Charles Robert Darwin and Robert Charles Winthrop wore their first diapers. And in a little log cabin in Hardin County, Kentucky, an illiterate laborer and his wife named their newborn son Abraham Lincoln. . . .

God is looking at your town, your city, your neighborhood, and He's looking for His people to whom He can say, "You are Mine. I want to use you there. Because you proved yourself faithful there."

CHARLES SWINDOLL
*David: A Man of Passion and Destiny*

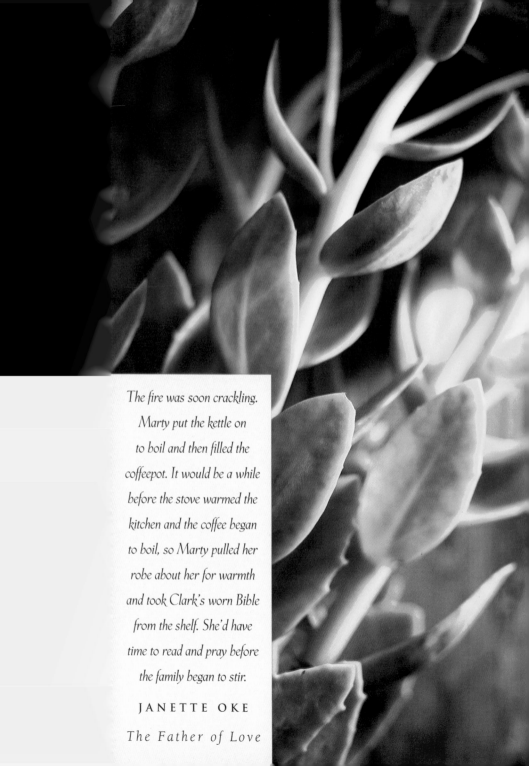

*The fire was soon crackling.*
*Marty put the kettle on*
*to boil and then filled the*
*coffeepot. It would be a while*
*before the stove warmed the*
*kitchen and the coffee began*
*to boil, so Marty pulled her*
*robe about her for warmth*
*and took Clark's worn Bible*
*from the shelf. She'd have*
*time to read and pray before*
*the family began to stir.*

JANETTE OKE

*The Father of Love*

# You Are Beautiful

*The LORD takes pleasure in His people;*
*He will beautify the humble with salvation.*

PSALM 149:4

When women come to know the Lord in a real and personal way, their frown lines begin to soften and worry creases start smoothing out. A sparkle appears in their eyes and a radiance falls over their countenance. . . .

When you allow the Lord to fill your heart with his boundless love, it shows on the outside. This beauty has nothing to do with cosmetics or plastic surgery. On the contrary, it's an inside–out job: A heart full of love produces a face full of joy.

When I stepped into a church for the first time as an adult, I was amazed to see pew after pew of attractive women. *Is this a requirement of membership?* I wondered. *Maybe they are all Mary Kay consultants. . . .* Soon I learned the happy truth: Such beauty is a gift from God. Unlike lipstick and mascara, which seldom last longer than a few hours, spiritual beauty is timeless. It literally pours out of your pores and alters your appearance in a most pleasing way. People will think you've had a facelift, when in fact you've had a *faith–lift!*

*Laughter is the sun that drives winter from the human face.*

BARBARA
JOHNSON

LIZ CURTIS HIGGS
*Reflecting His Image*

# Notes

❄

# Prayer Is Sabbath

---

*The LORD upholds all who fall,*
*and raises up all who are bowed down.*

PSALM 145:14

I believe our most honest, heartfelt prayers are the ones we pray in the middle of the night. Those prayers may not be very brave or noble or holy, but they come straight from the heart to God's ear. Lying in bed late at night with exhausted bodies and anxious minds, our usual, daily social defenses are all that's asleep. We are most open to God our Creator who knows our innermost thoughts, our most secret dreams. In the middle of the night, when we can't get off that anxious treadmill of worry and fear, the words "Please God, help!" form on our lips, take wing, and fly through the darkness.

Prayer is Sabbath. No matter what the actual content of our prayers, in prayer God calls us to trust him, to rest in him. When we pray, we lay down our burdens before the throne of Grace. Whether we pray for ourselves or others, we put ourselves or those for whom we pray to rest in God's hands. When we go into the bedroom and shut the door, we enter the Sabbath.

*Prayer is the language of intimacy and it transcends place and time.*

MADELEINE
L'ENGLE

HARRIET CROSBY
*A Place Called Home*

This morning we had our
first snowfall, and the world
was even more still, more
drawn into
itself as the sky fell.

KATHLEEN
NORRIS

*The Cloister
Walk*

## Bless My Good Intentions

❄

*I have loved you with an everlasting love;*
*therefore with lovingkindness I have drawn you.*

JEREMIAH 31:3

Lord, please bless my good intentions. I make so many promises to myself about all the nice things I'm going to do: Have somebody over. Phone, write, send books and get–well cards and flowers. . . .

You know my heart is full of love but also how full of other things is my day. Duties, demands, problems. So that, all too often, these other things don't get past my mental gates. Or are hopelessly blocked or detoured when they do.

The get–well cards I buy get lost—or I can't find the right address. The people I try to cheer up with a phone call are already on the phone, or out! . . . The cake I bake for the shut–in falls, or the car won't start to take it to her. . . .

They say hell is paved with good intentions, Lord. But I wonder if the paths to heaven aren't cobbled with them too?

*Getting things accomplished isn't nearly as important as taking time for love.*

JANETTE OKE

*Week 3*

MARJORIE HOLMES
*Lord, Let Me Love*

You can lift your spirits in
the bleak winter months by
filling your house with
blooming amaryllis, crocuses,
hyacinths, paper white
narcissus, freesias, and tulips.
Forcing bulbs—
coaxing flowers to bloom out
of their normal season—
is easy to do.

BARBARA MILO
OHRBACH

*Simply Flowers*

# When God Says No

❄

*My soul magnifies the Lord, and my spirit
has rejoiced in God my Savior.*

LUKE 1:46-47

There are times when the one thing you want is
the one doing you never get. . . . All you
want is an open door or an extra day or an
answered prayer, for which you will be thankful.

And so you pray and wait.

No answer.

You pray and wait.

No answer. . . .

May I ask a very important question? What if
God says no?

What if the request is delayed or even denied?
When God says no to you, how will you
respond? . . .

Test yourself with this question: What if God's only
gift to you were his grace to save you. Would you be
content? . . . You beg him to save the life of your child. You
plead with him to keep your business afloat. You implore him
to remove the cancer from your body. What if his answer is,
"My grace is enough." Would you be content?

You see, from heaven's perspective, grace is enough.

*Any path of sunlight in a dark
and deep woods could well be
described as a "path of
Godlight."*

TERRY LINDVALL

### MAX LUCADO
*In the Grip of Grace*

## The Offering of Myself

❊

*God is my salvation and my glory; the rock of my strength.*

PSALM 62:7

Years ago in a rural, Scottish village, the pastor of a small church was asked to resign. The ruling board of his congregation had evaluated the fruit of his ministry and could find nothing that seemed significant. No baptisms had been held the previous year, no conversions had been recorded, and only one response to a sermon could even be remembered.

That single response had taken place one Sunday when the offering plate had been passed. A small boy had put the plate on the floor then stepped into it. When asked for an explanation, he had replied that since he had no money to give God, he wanted to give himself.

The small boy who had stepped in the offering plate . . . became a great pioneer missionary–statesman used of God to change the course of individual lives, tribes, and nations in southern Africa. His name was Bobby Moffat. He was a man who overcame the smallness of his life by giving himself totally to God, keeping his focus on Christ.

ANNE GRAHAM LOTZ
*The Vision of His Glory*

## Goodness Costs

❄

*He who finds his life will lose it, and he who
loses his life for My sake will find it.*

MATTHEW 10:39

I t takes a lot to be good and gracious and generous
in a world where the mainstream of human
thinking moves in the opposite direction.

Generosity that is so much a part of goodness
is essentially a willingness to share what one has
with another. This reaches out to embrace all of
my life, not just my means. Generosity is much
more than merely sending a handsome check
to a charitable organization. It goes far beyond
giving to others out of my surplus and my
abundance.

When God, by His gracious Spirit, digs deeply
in the soil of my soul He will implant there the new,
divine impulse to be truly generous, truly self-giving.

This selfless self-sharing will entail more than just my
money. He will put His finger upon my time, talents, interests,
strength, energies, and capacities to enrich other lives. He will
ask me to set aside my own selfish self-interest in order to
give to others.

*Deep faith in action
is love, and love in
action is service.*

MOTHER TERESA

### PHILLIP KELLER
*The Inspirational Writings of Phillip Keller*

In the clear light of a winter's day, the
Liberon becomes a magnificent array
of grays, blues, and yellows. If you go
for a brisk walk in the afternoon you
can work up a warming glow, but as
soon as the sun dips down behind the
hills, you have to retreat back home.

On your return . . . you can take
refuge in the kitchen, warmed by a
bright burning fire and smelling
exquisitely of sugar, butter, and vanilla.
With rosy cheeks and eyes bright with
expectation, everyone is ready for a
delicious afternoon tea.

MICHEL BIEHN

*Recipes from a
Provençal Kitchen*

# The Extra-Ordinary

❄

*And this is the promise that He has promised us—eternal life.*

1 JOHN 2:25

"There is no event so commonplace but that God is present within it. . . " writes Frederick Buechner. No event so commonplace. A hidden God. A presence that steals into our lives like the season's first snowfall. So unlike the momentous, the pivotal, the turning points of our lives: receiving the diploma on graduation day, walking down the aisle toward the face of one we hope to grow old with at our wedding, pain giving way to joy in childbirth, the sudden tears as we are told a loved one didn't survive the surgery. Those are the momentous, the memorable, the transparent events that take us out of the ordinary. Those are the moments so few in each of our lives we can count them on one hand. If God only made his presence known in the momentous, how barren our lives would be of gracefilled windows to the sacred.

Instead, there are snowfalls and rain showers, waking and sleeping, as we live a succession of ordinary days. Into our ordinary world we are given this hidden God, one who comes to us as a baby born amid hay and barnyard smells to a nondescript couple on an ordinary night. Into the ordinary, came the extraordinary. The birth of a savior. And our lives will never be the same.

*The hope of the world lies in the Christmas message: Immanuel, God with us.*

JAMES
STEWART

❄

DEBRA KLINGSPORN
*Soul Searching*

### GOD'S MERRIMENT

"God rest you merry gentlemen . . ."
and in these pressured days
I, too, would seek to be so blessed
by Him, who still conveys
His merriment, along with rest.
So I would beg, on tired knees,
"God rest me merry,
this Christmas, please . . ."

## RUTH BELL GRAHAM
*Clouds Are the Dust of His Feet*

# God's Heart Revealed

❄

*Great peace have those who love Your law,*
*and nothing causes them to stumble.*

PSALM 119:165

We should do more than read [God's] words; we should seek "the Word exposed in the words," as Karl Barth said. We want to move beyond information to seeing God and being informed and shaped by His truth. . . .

Select a portion of Scripture—a verse, a paragraph, a chapter—and read it over and over. Think of Him as present and speaking to you, disclosing His mind and emotions and will. God is articulate. He speaks to us through His Word. Meditate on His words until His thoughts begin to take shape in your mind. . . .

When we read His Word we are reading His mind— what He knows, what He feels, what He wants, what He enjoys, what He desires, what He loves, what He hates.

DAVID ROPER
*Psalm 23*

*When we let God's Word seep into our lives little by little . . . it nourishes us and becomes a part of us.*

JANETTE OKE

❄

Time is not frozen. Time is never static. One day follows another. . . . Springtime planting precedes autumn harvest. Autumn's freezing of vegetables and making of jellies and jam precedes eating that food in front of a roaring fire as the snow blows against windows in the winter's storms.

EDITH
SCHAEFFER

*Common Sense
Christian Living*

# The Secret of a Pure Heart

❄

*Blessed are the pure in heart, for they shall see God.*

MATTHEW 5:8

Visiting in a mining town, a young minister was being escorted through one of the coal mines. In one of the dark, dirty passage-ways, he spied a beautiful white flower growing out of the black earth of the mine. "How can there be a flower of such purity and beauty in this dirty mine?" the minister asked the miner. "Throw some of the coal dust on it and see," was the reply. The minister did so and was surprised that as fast as the dirt touched those snowy petals, it slid right off to the ground, leaving the flower just as lovely as before. It was so smooth that the dirt could not cling to the flower.

Our hearts can be the same way. We cannot help it that we have to live in a world filled with sin, any more than the flower could change the place where it was growing. But God can keep us so pure and clean that though we touch sin on *every* side, it will not cling to us. We can stand in the midst of it just as white and beautiful as that flower. The secret of purity is God!

*God will never lead you where His strength cannot keep you.*

BARBARA
JOHNSON

❄

*Week 4*

BILLY GRAHAM
*The Secret of Happiness*

*It was the winter-wild,*
*While the heaven-born Child,*
*All meanly wrapt in the rude*
*manger lies;*
*Nature in awe to Him*
*Had doff'd her gaudy trim,*
*With her great Master so to*
*sympathize.*

JOHN MILTON
1608-1674

# Repeat the Sounding Joy

✳

*Those who sow in tears shall reap in joy.*

PSALM 126:5

To fail to praise is too frequently to fail to see the praiseworthy. . . . The humble one praises more frequently than the crank. The optimist celebrates the good more often than the pessimist. . . Those who complain and grumble find their mouths filled with toads and worms and rocks rather than the sweet, refreshing breath of praise.

Praise is simply appreciation made public. When we enjoy an experience fully, we burst into happy, spontaneous praise. And we invite others to join in that praise: "Wasn't that a great meal?" "Isn't she beautiful?" "Isn't this a surpris-ingly good book?" We urge others to add their instruments to our grand symphony of delight, to play and sing and laugh with us, because we believe in its delightfulness. Even our hymns of joy invite heaven and earth to sing and for that sounding joy to be repeated.

TERRY LINDVALL
*Surprised by Laughter*

*No matter where I am, no matter what obstacles I'm facing, I will seek the laughter in my winter.*

DEBRA
KLINGSPORN

# Christmas Snowfall

*I bring you good tidings of great joy, which shall be to all people.*

LUKE 2:10

I loved the snow of Christmas. It made the world look fit to welcome the King of kings even if He did come as a tiny baby and likely didn't even notice if there was snow or not. But I couldn't imagine Christmas without snow. Once when a visiting speaker at our church said that there most likely was no snow in Bethlehem on the night Jesus was born, I wanted to argue back that the fellow must be wrong. To think of Christmas with no snow—a dirty, bare, sordid world to welcome the Christ-Child—just didn't seem right.

Yes, I waited every year for a Christmas snowfall. It was like a hallowed sacrament to me—the covering of the drab, ugly world with clean freshness right from the hand of God Himself. The unclothed trees, the dirty rutted yard, the bare, empty fields—all were suddenly transformed into silvery, soft images, always making me think that something truly miraculous was happening before my eyes.

JANETTE OKE
*The Father of Love*

# A Mother's Heart

❄

*Blessed be the LORD God, the God of Israel,
who only does wondrous things!*

PSALM 72:18

**M**ary kept all these things, and pondered them in her heart. How many things a mother keeps, you think as you look about . . . Battered little first books. Baby shoes. Scrapbooks stuffed with their pictures and souvenirs. A daughter's first prom dress . . . Such foolish things that only a mother would cling to. All mothers, Mothers like Mary, who have gone before—and mothers to come. . . .

*The mystery and miracle of the incarnation makes every day a Christmas celebration for the believer.*

JANETTE OKE

You feel a renewed kinship for that girl–mother. You wonder what reminders of His childhood did she perhaps save. His first little garments, or the sandals in which He learned to walk? A wooden toy cart perhaps, that His father had made for him in the carpenter shop? And what memories did they bring back to her later to ponder in her heart? . . .

Christmas is for keeps. It comes every year and will go on forever. And along with Christmas belong the keepsakes and the customs. Those humble, everyday things that a mother clings to with her hands, and ponders, like Mary, in the secret spaces of her heart.

MARJORIE HOLMES
*Lord, Let Me Love*

On Christmas morning I
opened my grandmother's
present and saw, nestled in
tissue paper, the delicate pink
and white of her shell. I
picked it up and held it to my
ear, and there was the ocean,
murmuring. Outside, snow
was falling softly past the
window, but in the shell,
cupped in my hand, waves
lapped on a summer shore.

**FAITH ANDREWS
BEDFORD**

"My
Grandmother's
Shell"

# God—Our Dwelling Place

*If anyone loves Me, he will keep My word; and My Father will love him, and We will come to him and make Our home with him.*

JOHN 14:23

Your home is familiar to you. No one has to tell you how to locate your bedroom; you don't need directions to the kitchen. After a hard day scrambling to find your way around in the world, it's assuring to come home to a place you know. God can be equally familiar to you. With time you can learn where to go for nourishment, where to hide for protection, where to turn for guidance. . . .

God *wants* to be your dwelling place. He has no interest in being a weekend getaway or a Sunday bungalow or a summer cottage. Don't consider using God as a vacation cabin or an eventual retirement home. He wants you under his roof now and always. . . .

You may go days without thinking of him, but there's never a moment when he's not thinking of you.

*Teach us to escape the worries of this world, to live and rest in You.*

HARRIET
CROSBY

MAX LUCADO
*The Great House of God*

# Notes

❄

# A Day for Rest

❄

*He has made everything beautiful in its time.*

ECCLESIASTES 3:11

Sunrise, noon, sunset, midnight. Sunday, Monday, Tuesday, and Wednesday. January, May, September. Winter, spring, summer, autumn. Easter, Thanksgiving, Christmas. These are the punctuation marks of time, and what a marvelous mercy that God divided light from darkness, "and the evening and the morning were the first day.". . .

"For everything its season, and for every activity under heaven its time," wrote Qoholeth, the preacher of the book of Ecclesiastes. For birth, death, planting and uprooting, killing and healing, pulling down and building up, weeping and laughing, mourning and dancing, scattering stones and gathering them, embracing and refraining, seeking and losing, keeping and throwing away, tearing and mending. There are times for silence and speech, for love and hate, for war and peace.

For the Christian, time is transfigured as we see it held in the love of God, created by and for Jesus Christ, to whom belongs the primacy over all created things and who existed before everything and holds everything together.

*The higher your view of God, the higher your view of yourself.*

JAN
CARLBERG

ELISABETH ELLIOT
*Discipline: The Glad Surrender*

*After all the hustle and bustle of the holidays, it's sometimes easy to feel spiritually drained and dry. The psalmist sings that the one who meditates on God's law day and night is like a tree that never knows winter, planted as it is by streams of water.*

HARRIET
CROSBY

*A Well-Watered
Garden*

# A Spiritual Treasure Chest

❄

................................................. ❄ .................................................

*Your testimonies also are my delight and my counselors.*

PSALM 119:24

How do you feel when you find that wad of cash you hid in your sock drawer for safekeeping and forgot about? Or when you find the diamond that dropped out of your engagement ring? Or when you find the child who got away from you in the shopping mall and wandered out of your sight?

You rejoice. For each is a rich treasure, and finding it brings joy. But God's Word offers so much more.

Unlike any other treasure, it offers peace of mind to those who love and pursue it. Unlike any valuable, the Word of God gives strength, vigor, and energy to live without stumbling in weariness or fear.

Open your spiritual treasure chest today, and dig deep.

*In Scriptures,
even the little daisy
becomes a meadow.*

MARTIN LUTHER

# Week 5

## PETER WALLACE
*What the Psalmist Is Saying to You Today*

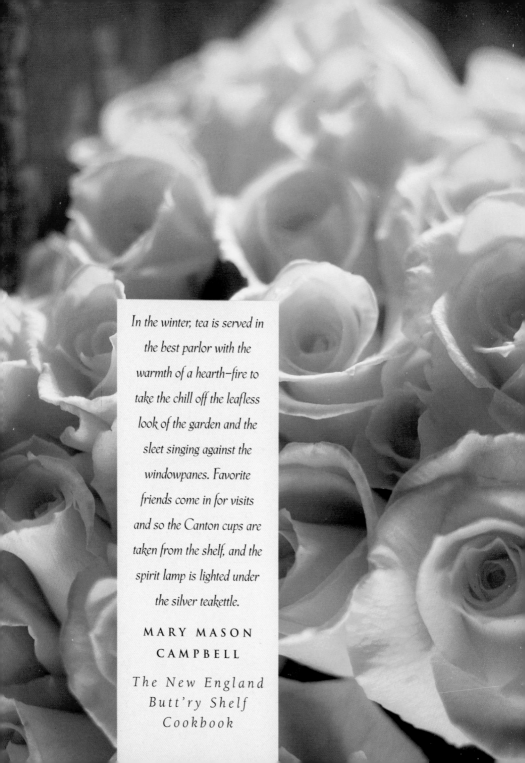

In the winter, tea is served in
the best parlor with the
warmth of a hearth–fire to
take the chill off the leafless
look of the garden and the
sleet singing against the
windowpanes. Favorite
friends come in for visits
and so the Canton cups are
taken from the shelf, and the
spirit lamp is lighted under
the silver teakettle.

MARY MASON
CAMPBELL

*The New England
Butt'ry Shelf
Cookbook*

# Advertising the Christian Life

❄

*This is the victory that has overcome the world—our faith.*

1  J O H N   5 : 4

I thought it would be interesting to look at American advertising in light of the beatitudes. American products claim, openly or covertly, a variety of miracles for those who purchase their goods. Buy aspirin and get rid of pain. Buy weight-loss products and get good looks. . . . Buy beverages and get friends, popularity. The ideal American life as portrayed in our ads is a pain-free existence with the self-image of our choice, emphasizing sex appeal, youth, and popularity— all based on the physical world, and all obtained from products which can be bought with money.

What about the spiritual life? If Jesus were on TV today advertising what He has to offer, what would a commercial for the ideal spiritual life be like? According to Luke 6, Jesus promotes the following characteristics: poverty, hunger, weeping, being hated. Matthew 5 continues the list: mourning, meekness, mercy, pureness in heart, peacemaking, being persecuted.

Can you imagine how an ad for these qualities would run? What Jesus wants of us is not the American dream.

*Spend one hour a day in adoration of the Lord and you'll be all right.*

MOTHER  TERESA

L E S L I E   W I L L I A M S
*Night Wrestling*

# The Requirement

❄

*Yet in all these things we are more than*
*conquerors through Him who loved us.*

ROMANS 8:37

The headmistress of the boarding school I attended used to say, "Don't go around with a Bible under your arm if you don't sweep under the bed." She was looking for a genuine faith, which is always a practical faith. She wanted no spiritual talk coming out of a messy room. . . .

During Jesus' three years as an itinerant rabbi He knew what it was to be weary, hungry, and homeless. The common people heard Him gladly but the religious elite could not stand Him. He was misquoted, misjudged, misrepresented, misunderstood. . . . He had every reason to feel lonely in the world of men, but it was thus that He "learned" and demonstrated for us the meaning of obedience—through the things that He suffered. . . .

To walk with Him is to walk the Way of the Cross. If the cross we are asked to take up is not presented to us in the form of martyrdom, heroic action of some kind, dragons or labyrinths or even "ministry"—at least something that looks spiritual—are we to conclude that He has waived the requirement?

He never waives the requirement.

ELISABETH ELLIOT
*The Path of Loneliness*

## Waiting in Stillness

❄

*The work of righteousness will be peace, and the effect of righteousness, quietness and assurance forever.*

ISAIAH 32:17

The first thing you notice on a snowy morning is the stillness. Even in the city, there is a difference. Sounds are muffled. Not everything that normally moves is able to move, and what is in motion goes more slowly. Snowfall is a summons to slow down, to live more in time than against it, to relax and to take account of our surroundings.

Winter's snow and ice restrain us, require us to reconsider priorities and take more time. . . .

In the country or the woods, the stillness of winter becomes profound. Streams and ponds and lakes cease to move. Animals hibernate. . . . If we move, the squeaky crunch of snow under our own boots is the only sound. When we stand, the silence radiates as far as we can hear. . . . Waiting in stillness, we hear the absence of sound become the presence of the voice of God. The utter silence speaks the Creator's first and simplest benediction: It is good.

*Happiness is not a right to be grasped, but a serendipity to be enjoyed.*

RICHARD J. FOSTER

DAVID RENSBERGER
*"The Holiness of Winter"*

*Sleeping on the hearth of
the living world,
yawning at home before the
fire of life
feeling the presence of the
living God
like a great
reassurance
a deep calm in the heart
a presence. . . .*

D. H.
LAWRENCE

1885-1930

# Redefining Success

❄

*Draw near to God, and He will draw near to you.*

JAMES 4:8

Perhaps nothing diverts us from focused living more than our concept of success. Published studies inform us of what conveys power in body language, business lunches, and the cars we drive. We "dress for success." Society is not only preoccupied with the image of success, but for the most part is dependent on someone else to define success. . . .

Was Jesus successful? He had no home of his own. The successful people of His day viewed Him skeptically, if not with hostility. His followers were a ragtag bunch without social or political influence. And even this motley crew fell away as He approached the Cross. None of His disciples accompanied Him in His darkest hour. He had neither wealth, political power, or unusual physical beauty. . . .

Jesus measured His own success by one criterion: "I came . . . not to do my will but to do the will of him who sent me" (John 6:38). "I finished the work."

### JEAN FLEMING
*Finding Focus in a Whirlwind World*

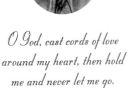

*O God, cast cords of love around my heart, then hold me and never let me go.*

PURITAN
PRAYER

❄

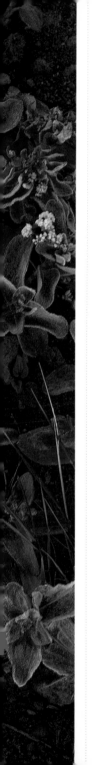

# Notes

❄

## Enthroned in Beauty

---- ❄ ----

*Nevertheless I am continually with You:*
*You hold me by my right hand.*

PSALM 73:23

In the Old Testament, when the high priest went into the Most Holy Place once a year to sprinkle the blood of the lamb on the mercy seat to make atonement for sin, he wore a breastplate that covered his heart and chest. . . . The breastplate was encrusted with twelve stones, each one carved with one of the names of the tribes of Israel. Wearing this breastplate signified that when the high priest went into God's presence, he carried the names of God's children on his heart. The first of those stones was a carnelian. And the last was a jasper.

When John described the One Who sat on the throne, he said He "had the appearance of jasper and carnelian" (Rev. 4:3a). A jasper was a clear stone, much like a diamond. A carnelian, or sardus stone, had more the color of a ruby. . . . It is as though John was describing God saying, even by the colors He wore, "I love you. I love you. I love you. I carry you by name on My heart forever." When seated on the throne at the center of the universe, preparing to judge the world, Jesus gives you and me evidence we are on His heart!

*The heart which has no agenda but God's is the heart at leisure from itself.*

ELISABETH
ELLIOT

❄

ANNE GRAHAM LOTZ
*The Vision of His Glory*

Snow comes by night—a
quiet magic. A secret
tiptoeing down while people
sleep. . . . Snow comes by
night, to fill grown-ups with
wonder, and children with
enchantment.

MARJORIE
HOLMES

*Love and
Laughter*

Winter and Summer,
  glorify the Lord.
Glorify the Lord, O chill and
  cold, Drops of dew
and flakes of snow.
Frost and cold, ice and sleet,
  Glorify the Lord.

**THE BOOK OF
COMMON PRAYER**

# Follow the Right Path

❊

*You are my rock and my fortress: therefore,*
*for Your name's sake, lead me and guide me.*

PSALM 31:3

God made us originally like Himself, and when the human race fell into willful disobedience, we all lost something. We lost the clear-cut lines of the original image of God's character stamped on our spiritual features. We lost the desire to glorify Him. God wants to restore that original image in our lives. . . .

My mother loves antiques. She was always busy restoring some old chunk of wood—or so it appeared to us. But when her work was finished, the image that had been hidden emerged, bringing forth admiration and praise. To *fail successfully* means to decide that He must be allowed to complete His restoring work in our lives *for His name's sake;* to fail to follow, and to try, try again, until we find ourselves succeeding means that, in the end, our lives will give praise and appreciation to Him. After all, the whole duty of man is to bring glory to God.

*The Christian journey is the process of learning to accept Christ's outstretched hand as He leads us down the sometimes mucky road of life.*

LESLIE WILLIAMS
❊

# Week 6

JILL BRISCOE
*How to Follow the Shepherd*

A flowering plant brings a
breath of spring into the
home in winter.

BARBARA MILO
OHRBACH

*Simply Flowers*

# The Prayer of Helplessness

❄

*This hope we have as an anchor of the soul,
both sure and steadfast.*

HEBREWS 6:19

My most spectacular answers to prayers have come when I was helpless, so out of control as to be able to do nothing at all for myself. . . .

Why would God insist on helplessness as a prerequisite to answered prayer? One obvious reason is that our human helplessness is bedrock fact. God is a realist and insists that we be realists too. So long as we are deluding ourselves that human resources can supply our heart's desires, we are believing a lie. . . .

Did Jesus have any comment about all this? Yes, as always He put His finger on the very heart of the matter: "Without me ye can do nothing" (John 15:5). . . .

Yet not only did Jesus insist on the truth of our helplessness; He underscored it by telling us that this same helplessness applied equally to Him while He wore human flesh: "The Son can do nothing of himself, but what he seeth the Father do" (John 5:19). In this as in everything else, He was setting the pattern for imperfect humanity.

*I ask great things
of a great God.*

PURITAN
PRAYER

## CATHERINE MARSHALL
*Adventures in Prayer*

# Extravagant Giving

❄

*Blessed are those who do His commandments, that they may have the right to the tree of life, and may enter through the gates into the city.*

REVELATION 22:14

When Jesus watched the voluntary offerings made in the temple treasury, he was moved by the sacrificial gift of the poor widow. What was it about her giving that touched him so? Jesus' comment on that simple act was, "For they all contributed out of their abundance; but she out of her poverty has put in everything she had, her whole living" (Mark 12:44).

Her giving had a certain reckless abandon to it. She evidenced an undivided devotion that fulfilled the command to love God with all the heart, soul, mind, and strength. In fact, in Mark's Gospel this story follows closely on the heels of the two great commandments, as if to be a commentary upon them. A simple act, but one that crystallized the Christian witness. Here was a woman free from idolatry to mammon, devoid of greed and avarice. Here was a person in whom extravagant giving exceeded prudent thrift. Here was a widow, helpless and defenseless, who had learned to trust the Father in heaven for her needs day by day, one who sought first the Kingdom of God and his righteousness. Dare we follow her lead?

RICHARD J. FOSTER
*Freedom of Simplicity*

# Created in God's Likeness

❄

*For we are members of His body, of His flesh and of His bones.*

EPHESIANS 5:30

Repentance is homecoming. To repent is to stop traveling away from God and to return to be cleansed in the grace and mercy of Jesus Christ. But we don't return home empty-handed. We bring God the gift of our humanity, which bears Christ's image. God loves us because we are human beings created in his image. . . .

While God loves us because we are human, the world despises our humanity. Our culture bombards us with the message that simply being human is not enough. Advertising constantly tells us we are not beautiful enough, not sexy enough, not healthy enough, not clean enough, not happy enough, not young enough, not successful enough, not powerful enough, not well-dressed enough. . . .

In our world, human beings are dehumanized by the numbers. But Jesus calls each one by name. "Of how much more value are you than the birds!"

What in the world does God see in us anyway? He sees human beings. He sees the cross. He sees Jesus.

*God's love in the face of our sin is what causes us to long for His righteousness.*

DAVID ROPER

HARRIET CROSBY
*A Place Called Home*

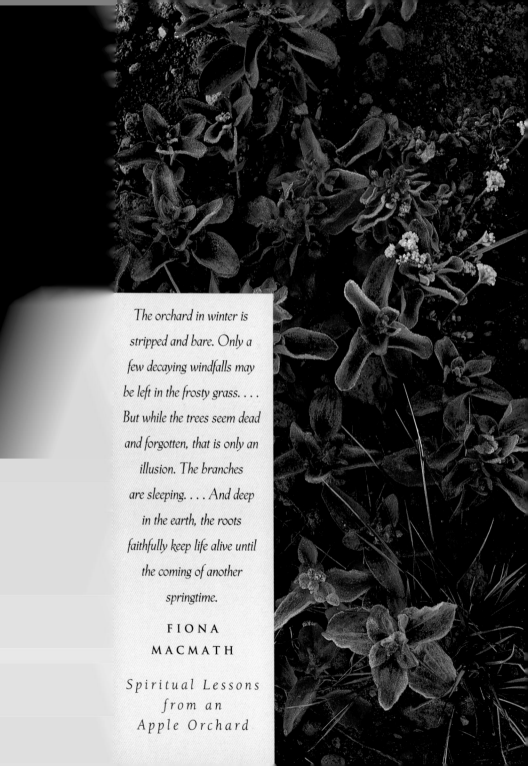

The orchard in winter is
stripped and bare. Only a
few decaying windfalls may
be left in the frosty grass. . . .
But while the trees seem dead
and forgotten, that is only an
illusion. The branches
are sleeping. . . . And deep
in the earth, the roots
faithfully keep life alive until
the coming of another
springtime.

FIONA
MACMATH

*Spiritual Lessons
from an
Apple Orchard*

# The Common Thread in Our Garments

※

*I can do all things through Christ who strengthens me.*

PHILIPPINES 4:13

We don't look alike. We don't act alike. We don't dress alike. We have different tastes in the food we eat, the books we read, the cars we drive, and the music we enjoy. You like opera; I like country. We have dissimilar backgrounds, goals, and motivations. We work at different jobs, and we enjoy different hobbies....We have our own unique convictions on child-rearing and education. Our weights vary. Our heights vary. So does the color of our skin.

But there is one thing we all have in common: We all know what it means to hurt.

Suffering is a universal language. Tears are the same for Jews or Muslims or Christians, for white or black or brown, for children or adults or the elderly. When life hurts and our dreams fade, we may express our anguish in different ways, but each one of us knows the sting of pain and heartache, disease and disaster, trials and sufferings....

God has given us a purpose for our existence, a reason to go on, even though that existence includes tough times. Living through suffering, we become sanctified—in other words, set apart for the glory of God. We gain perspective. We grow deeper. We grow up!

*Christianity teaches righteousness, not rights.*

ELISABETH ELLIOT

※

## CHARLES SWINDOLL
*Hope Again*

# Notes

· · · · · · · · · · · · · · · · · · · · · · · ❄ · · · · · · · · · · · · · · · · · · · · · · · ·

# A Fire Within

❄

*In the fear of the LORD there is strong confidence,*
*and His children will have a place of refuge.*

PROVERBS 14:26

God reveals his will by setting a torch to your soul. He gave Jeremiah a fire for hard hearts. He gave Nehemiah a fire for a forgotten city. He set Abraham on fire for a land he'd never seen. . . .

And isn't there one within you? Want to know God's will for your life? Then answer this question, "What ignites your heart?" Forgotten orphans? Untouched nations? The inner city? The outer limits?

Heed the fire within! Do you have a passion to sing? Then sing!

Are you stirred to manage? Then manage!

Do you ache for the ill? Then treat them!

Do you hurt for the lost? Then teach them!

Mark it down: Jesus comes to set you on fire! He walks as a torch from heart to heart warming the cold and thawing the chilled and stirring the ashes. He is at once a Galilean wildfire and a welcome candle. He comes to purge infection and illuminate your direction.

The fire of your heart is the light of your path.

*The Christian life is no less than Christ's own life struggling to show itself from inside us.*

MICHAEL GREEN

❄

## MAX LUCADO
*The Great House of God*

*It is an old French country*
*custom to put a bowl of*
*fragrant lemons or limes in a*
*guest room to purify the air.*

BARBARA MILO
OHRBACH

*Simply Flowers*

# Shine Up Your Neighbor's Halo

❄

*The glory which You gave Me, I have given them, that they may
be one just as We are one: I in them, and You in Me.*

JOHN 17:22 — 23

One Sunday morning, drowsing in a back pew of a little country church, I dimly heard the old preacher urge his flock to "stop worrying about your own halo and shine up your neighbor's!" And it left me sitting up, wide-awake, because it struck me as just about the best eleven-word formula for getting along with people that I ever heard.

*Only as we know how much God
loves each of us can we begin to
know how to love each other.*

DAVID A. HUBBARD

I like it for its implication that everyone, in some area of life, has a halo that's worth watching for and acknowledging. I like it for the droll celestial picture it conjures up: Everybody industriously polishing away at everybody else's little circle of divine light. I like it for the firm way it shifts the emphasis from self to interest and concern for others. Finally, I like it because it reflects a deep psychological truth: People have a tendency to become what you expect them to be.

## Week 7

ARTHUR GORDON
*A Touch of Wonder*

*Lord, let me keep my rejoicing current. As fresh as the eggs, as new as the morning paper, as bright as my children's faces or the sunlight dancing at the door.*

MARJORIE
HOLMES

*Lord,
Let Me Love*

# Walking and Talking with God

❄

*I have set the LORD always before me;*
*because He is at my right hand I shall not be moved.*

PSALM 16:8

My first observation of perfectly natural and conscientious prayer came when I was a very little girl in Shanghai. One morning I went skipping along beside Dr. Hoste, at that time the director of the China Inland Mission (he had followed Hudson Taylor). He didn't turn me away, but simply said, "Edith, I am praying now, but you may come along if you wish."

I walked with him a number of times, holding his hand and being very quiet and impressed as he prayed aloud. It was his custom to walk when he prayed, and he counted it his first responsibility for the mission to pray four hours a day. He prayed for each missionary in the China Inland Mission, and for each of their children by name. . . .

"All right, walk with me and pray," he would say in his peculiarly high voice. The impression that penetrates my memory is the respect I received for the *work* of prayer. I know it meant more than any series of lectures in later life could mean.

*Prayer is like incense. It costs a great deal.*

ELISABETH
ELLIOT

EDITH SCHAEFFER
*Common Sense Christian Living*

# A Trail of Gladness

· · · · · · · · · · · · · · · · · · · · · ❄ · · · · · · · · · · · · · · · · · · · · ·

*Let the beauty of the LORD our God be upon us,*
*and establish the work of our hands.*

PSALM 90:17

On one occasion two friends spent a few days in our home while passing through en route to some engagements in the East. They invited me to go along. After several days on the road one of the men missed his hat. He was sure it had been left in our home. He asked me to write my wife to find it and kindly send it on to him.

Her letter of reply was one I shall never forget. One sentence in particular made an enormous impact on me. "I have combed the house from top to bottom and can find no trace of the hat. The only thing those men left behind was a great blessing!"

Is this the way people feel about me? Do I leave a trail of sadness or of gladness behind? . . . "Do I leave behind for-giveness—or bitterness?" "Do I leave behind contentment—or conflict?" "Do I leave behind flowers of joy—or frustration?" "Do I leave behind love—or rancor?"

PHILLIP KELLER
*The Inspirational Writings of Phillip Keller*

## *Filled with God Himself*

✳

*You shall be a blessing. Do not fear, let your hands be strong.*

ZECHARIAH 8:13

When have you observed the blazing glory of a tropical sunset or the soft, silvery shimmer of moonlight on the ocean waves,

> or a baby's birth and first lusty cry,
> or a bird weaving her nest, hatching and feeding her young,
> or an exquisite lady's-slipper tucked into a rocky crevice in the forest,
> or a hummingbird suspended in air,
> or a V-shaped flight of geese migrating north,
> or the blinding flash of a jagged bolt of lightening splitting the darkness. . . .

When we thoughtfully consider the world around us, we instinctively know our environment is not some haphazard cosmic accident but the handiwork of a Master Designer. . . . Like Planet Earth around us, our lives are not a haphazard cosmos either. They were deliberately planned to be filled with the beauty of love and joy and peace and purpose—with God Himself.

*God makes His heart visible to, then through, you.*

JAN CARLBERG

ANNE GRAHAM LOTZ
*The Glorious Dawn of God's Story*

One of the great pleasures in
winter is human community.
Two people in love huddle
together for warmth.
A family gathers around a
bright table on a dark night.
Friends share a fire
and a pot of tea.

**DAVID
RENSBERGER**

*"The Holiness
of Winter"*

# A God-Dappled Day

✻

*I know the thoughts that I think toward you, says the LORD,*
*thoughts of peace and not of evil, to give you a future and a hope.*

JEREMIAH 29:11

I f we train ourselves, we can sense God's presence in every object or person we encounter during even a humdrum day; and recognizing the sparkle in the bubble is itself a way to worship the God who created bubbles and added sparkles for the fun of it.

An ideally God-dappled day would begin, as do other days, when the alarm clock unseats us from our dreams. Instead of groaning, sighing, lugging my creaking carcass from the cozy blankets, a more disciplined Christian might take the opportunity to thank God for a sense of hearing, . . . letting my body tingle with the news that I woke up. *I have been granted another day.*

Just like training for any sport, learning to feel beyond the physical takes discipline. I try to take inventory at the end of the day, asking God to penetrate my world, to make the ordinary gleam. With practice and conscious effort, we can all find God in the most surprising places: in patterns of tree bark, in sunsets reflected off skyscrapers, in the steam of hot amaretto coffee.

*We can count blessings, or we can count calamities.*

BARBARA
JOHNSON

## LESLIE WILLIAMS
*Night Wrestling*

# Notes

❄

# Time Out for Love

❄

*Your words have upheld him who was stumbling,*
*and you have strengthened the feeble knees.*

JOB 4:4

Lord, don't ever let me be too busy to love . . . A child who comes running in for a hug and lavish exclamations of praise because he's just learned to stand on his head. Yea, though I'm trying to make bouillabaisse . . . don't let me shoo him away.

Don't let me be too busy to love, Lord . . . A neighbor who's just had a fight with her husband and needs a shoulder to cry on. . . .

Lord, don't let me be too busy to love . . . My husband when he's tired and discouraged, or high from a big deal at the office, or simply wants my attention. . . .

And now, Lord, thank you for giving me so many people, so many opportunities to love. But please forgive me when I fail them; help them to forgive me, and me to forgive myself. You made me human, and there is only so much of me to go around.

MARJORIE HOLMES
*Lord, Let Me Love*

*People with time*
*for others are happy*
*all around the clock.*

BARBARA
JOHNSON

❄

*Father in Heaven,*

*Deliver me from carking
care, and make me a happy,
holy person; . . . Teach me to
laud, adore, and magnify
thee, with the music of
heaven, And make me a
perfume of praiseful
gratitude to thee.*

**PURITAN
PRAYER**

*The Valley
of Vision*

# Let Us Glorify Him

❄️

*Surely the righteous shall give thanks to Your name;
the upright shall dwell in Your presence.*

PSALM 140:13

The obvious meaning of the word *glorify* is "to give homage to, as in worship." But there is a deeper meaning. Dr. Leslie Weatherhead in a 1952 Lenten sermon in the City Temple, London, brought out this richer meaning: "I would define glory as that expression of the nature of a person or thing which, of itself, evokes our praise."

Then the "glory" of a sunrise must be in the beauty of its delicate pinks and oranges reflected in the sky just before the sun itself appears. . . .

The "glory" of Jesus Christ lies in the characteristics of His nature that make us want to adore Him. These traits are not kingly trappings or the halo placed around His head by medieval painters. Far from it! Men and women saw His glory in His humanity—His instant compassion, tenderness, understanding . . . His ultimate self-giving on the cross.

*God is at the center of the universe, and at the center of our quest.*

LESLIE WILLIAMS

❄️

# Week 8

CATHERINE MARSHALL
*The Best of Catherine Marshall*

The baked apple is the
elephant rag doll of desserts:
ugly and wrinkled, but sweet
and well-loved.

HELEN
GUSTAFSON

*The Agony of
the Leaves*

# *Like a Subtle Perfume*

*When you walk, your steps will not be hindered,
and when you run, you will not stumble.*

PROVERBS 4:12

There's something winsome and wonderfully compelling about those whom God is making strong. They're easier to get along with, easier to work with and live with, more gentle and genial. Their goodness is like old wine—mellow and fragrant. They have a profound and bewildering effect upon others. Their actions keep reminding people of . . . well, of God.

That sort of influence cannot be conjured up or contrived. It's not a matter of feminine force or male machismo; it's not a function of self-assertiveness, intellect, charisma, charm, or chutzpah. It *happens*—the fruit of our association with God. . . .

When we try to be influential we become aggressive and intrusive. We crowd people and push them away from the truth. . . . But those whom God is making good are powerfully persuasive. They have a fragrance like a subtle perfume. Wherever they go, they leave behind the unforgettable aroma of their Lord (2 Corinthians 2:14–17).

*God sets His heart of favor
on those whose hearts are
following him.*

CHARLES
SWINDOLL

DAVID ROPER
*Psalm 23*

## No Regrets

❄

*May the Lord direct your hearts into the love*
*of God and into the patience of Christ.*

2 THESSALONIANS 3:5

Christians think and act within the framework of
eternity. They are not embittered when things
don't turn out the way they planned. They know
that the sufferings of this present world are not worthy to be
compared with the glory that shall be revealed hereafter. So
rejoice and be exceedingly glad! . . .

When Bill Borden, son of the wealthy Bordens, left for
China as a missionary, many of his friends thought he was
foolish to "waste his life," as they put it, trying to convert a
few heathen to Christianity. But Bill loved Christ and he loved
people! On his way to China he contracted a disease and died.
At his bedside they found a note that he had written while he
was dying. It read: "No reserve, no retreat, and no regrets."

Borden had found more happiness in his few years of
sacrificial service than most people find in a lifetime.

BILLY GRAHAM
*The Secret of Happiness*

# Grace in a Barren Place

*Keep yourselves in the love of God, looking for the mercy of our Lord Jesus Christ unto eternal life.*

JUDE 21

We refer to a ballet dancer as having grace. We say grace at meals. We talk about the queen of England bringing grace to events she attends. Grace can mean coordination of movement, it can mean a prayer, it can refer to dignity and elegance. Most importantly, grace can mean unmerited favor—extending special favor to someone who doesn't deserve it, who hasn't earned it, and can never repay it.

Some of you can look back to a time when you were addicted to drugs, when you were involved in a futile life, moving from one skirmish to another. . . . You offered nothing to God. You had nothing that you could give to Him, not one good work that you could say genuinely revealed righteousness. And yet the King set His heart on you. Isn't that great? . . . There's something freeing about grace. It takes away all of the demands and it puts all of the response on God's shoulders as He comes to us and says, "You're Mine. I take you just as you are . . . hang-ups and liabilities, and all."

*No sin is great enough to drain dry the ocean of God's grace.*

ELISABETH
ELLIOT

## CHARLES SWINDOLL
*David: A Man of Passion and Destiny*

As long as the earth endures,
seedtime and harvest, cold
and heat, summer and winter;
day and night, shall not cease.

GENESIS 8:22
N R S V

# *You Are Valuable*

❄

*And let us consider one another
in order to stir up love and good works.*

HEBREWS 10:24

How do you measure your value? Dollars in the bank? Cars in the driveway? Letters after your name? During the Depression, you were something special if you had a little meat on your bones. That meant you were prosperous, that nobody at *your* house was starving. People could see you were well cared for, and for that matter, cared about.

Well, suppose we...look at the birds of the air. Have you ever seen a skinny bird? Maybe if it was sickly and couldn't fly off to find food, but the ones in the air are plump and healthy and flying high. Even though they have no food stored up for tomorrow, they seem to be doing fine today on the food that their heavenly Father has provided....And Jesus said we are of *more* value to God than those happily fed birds, meaning he will look out for *all* our needs, not just physical, but spiritual needs too.

*O Lord, teach me that if I do not live a life that satisfies thee, I shall not live a life that will satisfy me.*

PURITAN PRAYER

❄

LIZ CURTIS HIGGS
*Reflecting His Image*

# Notes

❄

# A Happy Habit

❄

*The LORD is near to all who call upon Him,*
*to all who call upon Him in truth.*

PSALM 145:18

I t is always possible to be thankful for what is given
rather than to complain about what is not given.
One or the other becomes a habit of life.

Many women have told me that my husband's
advice, which I once quoted in a book, has been an
eye–opener to them. He said that a wife, if she is
very generous, may allow that her husband lives
up to perhaps eighty percent of her expectations.
There is always the other twenty percent that she
would like to change, and she may chip away at it
for the whole of their married life without reduc–
ing it by very much. She may, on the other hand,
simply decide to enjoy the eighty percent, and both of
them will be happy. It's a down–to–earth illustration of
a principle: Accept, positively and actively, what is given. Let
thanksgiving be the habit of your life.

Such acceptance is not possible without a deep and abiding
belief in the sovereign love of God. Either he is in charge, or
he is not. Either he loves us, or he does not. If he is in charge
and loves us, then whatever is given is subject to his control
and is meant ultimately for our joy.

*To the heart that is attuned*
*to Him, God comes in*
*surprising ways.*

HENRY
GARIEPY

ELISABETH ELLIOT
*Love Has a Price Tag*

Winter is a time of quietness
and reflection, a time of
"nesting" while much of the
earth sleeps and waits for
spring. Winter is the
contemplative season.
It invites us to sit by the
hearth and dream about
God, to shift our focus from
creation to the Creator.

HARRIET
CROSBY

*A Well-Watered
Garden*

# Simple Gratitude

❄

*Praise the LORD of hosts, for the LORD is good,*
*for His mercy endures forever.*

JEREMIAH 33:1

Being grateful is no Pollyanna-like response to anxious times. For most of us, the daily practice of gratitude begins at mealtimes. For many households, it is not necessarily the calmest, most serene time of day. Frazzled from working all day, Mom has to come up with a healthy, nutritious meal in less than thirty minutes. Dad isn't in such great shape himself; after the stress of the office, he tries to maintain order among fussy, hungry kids. When everyone finally sits down to supper, Sis is sulky, the baby's bawling, and her brother is trying to tell everybody about his day at school, two decibels above his baby sister. "Let us now be thankful. . . ." Right.

*Almighty God, may my lips be a well-tuned harp to sound Thy praise.*

PURITAN PRAYER

❄

But that's where real gratitude begins. Not when life is peaceful and serene, but when everything's falling apart and the resulting anxiety is enough to drive you right through your eyeballs. For anxious people, being grateful to God is a miracle. Simple gratitude helps us experience God at work in every moment of every day.

*Week 9*

HARRIET CROSBY
*A Place Called Home*

*A room is transformed*
*when you introduce*
*something green and*
*growing. . . . Suddenly, it*
*becomes warmer, friendlier,*
*more comfortable—a room*
*where people love to be.*

BARBARA MILO
OHRBACH

*Simply Flowers*

# Delightful Diversity

*For we are His workmanship, created in Christ Jesus for good works, which God prepared beforehand that we should walk in them.*

EPHESIANS 2:10

There are some 2,500 varieties of apple in the British National collection, and a similar number in the New York State collection, each with different habits, colors, flavors, scents, and sweetnesses. Some would be worth growing for their beautiful names alone: in England the Reinette, Orange Pippin . . . Beauty of Bath, D'Arcy Spice; in North America the Maiden's Blush, Northern Spy, Winesap, and Wolf River. . . .

The apostle Paul exhorts his brothers and sisters in Corinth to value each other for their variety of gifts. Such variety comes from God, who delights to create in a myriad of forms. Variety is precious. Do not seek to impose uniformity on others, for they are individuals, endowed with different characteristics and gifts, and precious in God's sight.

Further, do not expect of yourself all the gifts that you admire in others. Each variety is valuable for itself, and we don't look for anything beyond natural perfection in each apple of its kind. Neither should we expect in ourselves the full perfection of opposites. If we do, disappointment is inevitable.

*There is divine purpose in bringing out the best in one another.*

DENIS WAITLEY

FIONA MACMATH
*Spiritual Lessons from an Apple Orchard*

# A God of Paradox

❄

*Now godliness with contentment is great gain.*

1 TIMOTHY 6:6

Salvation. Frederick Buechner says, "It is a process, not an event." I find that disconcerting. I want an event, something like Christmas. I want a grand and glorious once-and-for-all event.

This God of seasons and stages, life and death, cold and warmth; this God of contrasts and paradox; this is not a God of easy answers and ready reassurance. I want a once-and-for-all god. The kind that makes you go through something once, and you don't have to go through it again. Once you've tasted the salty sting from tears of grief, you can dry your eyes, blow your nose and say, "Okay, God, I've done that once. I don't have to do that again." I want the kind of faith that once you figure out what it is, you don't have to keep wrestling with it. The kind that once you say, "Okay, God, I'll give you my life," you don't have to keep learning what giving it to him actually means. . . .

If I had salvation or faith or God Himself once—and—for—all, I would probably forget it (or him) tomorrow. I can only live this one day and experience the saving grace of God within this present moment.

DEBRA KLINGSPORN
*Soul Searching*

# A Plate Full of Experiences

*My food is to do the will of Him who sent Me,*
*and to finish His work.*

JOHN 4:34

L ast night during family devotions. I called my
daughters to the table and set a plate in front
of each. In the center of the table I
placed a collection of food: some fruit, some
raw vegetables, and some Oreo cookies. "Every
day," I explained, "God prepares for us a plate
of experiences. What kind of plate do you most
enjoy?"

The answer was easy. Sara put three cookies
on her plate. Some days are like that, aren't they?
Some days are "three cookie days." Many are not.
Sometimes our plate has nothing but vegetables—
twenty-four hours of celery, carrots, and squash.
Apparently God knows we need some strength, and
though the portion may be hard to swallow, isn't it for our
own good? Most days, however, have a bit of it all. Vegetables,
which are healthy but dull. Fruit, which tastes better and we
enjoy. And even an Oreo, which does little for our nutrition,
but a lot for our attitude. . . .

*God deserves singleness*
*of heart because*
*He is God!*

JAN CARLBERG

The next time your plate has more broccoli than apple pie,
remember who prepared the meal. And the next time your
plate has a portion you find hard to swallow, talk to God
about it. Jesus did.

MAX LUCADO
*The Great House of God*

I can almost smell the toasty
aromas of popcorn or a pie
baking. I can hear the lively
sounds of laughter and
perhaps the tinkle of a music
box. . . . And I see it all lit
by the golden glow of a
fireplace or a candle or a
lamp with a fringed shade.

**THOMAS
KINKADE**

*Simpler Times*

# Expensive Words

❄

*Before they call, I will answer;*
*and while they are still speaking, I will hear.*

ISAIAH 65:24

One lesson I tried to teach my children from an early age, repeating over and over again ... was the fact that some things must never be said, no matter how hot the argument, no matter how angry one becomes, no matter how far one goes in feeling, "I don't care how much I hurt him [or her]." Some things are too much of a "luxury" ever to say. Some things are too great a price to pay for the momentary satisfaction of cutting the other person down. Some things are like throwing indelible ink on a costly work of art, or smashing a priceless statue just to make a strong point in an argument. Saying certain things is an expense beyond all reason. This is true for man, woman, and child. Proverbs says something in this direction which applies whether it is the mother or father, grandparents or aunts and uncles, children who are brothers and sisters, or cousins speaking to each other. "Every wise woman buildeth her house: but the foolish plucketh it down with her hands. . . . In the mouth of the foolish is a rod of pride: but the lips of the wise shall preserve them" (14:1, 3).

*Respect is a habit*
*that is developed*
*daily in little ways.*

SUSAN YATES

EDITH SCHAEFFER
*What Is a Family?*

# Notes

❄

# Holiness in Hidden Places

❄

*By the breath of God ice is given, and the broad waters are frozen.*

JOB 37:10

In winter, when the world is simplified, the subtler and humbler beauties can appear to us. White snow and the dull grays and browns of winter vegetation let anything with a bit of color show up more clearly. Red holly berries, or rose hips on their dry canes, or the enduring green of pine trees call us to closer observation. Even a blue jay stands out. The simplicity and starkness of a winter scene bring to our attention creatures we overlook in other seasons. The beauty of such small and humble things is an especially important expression of holiness for us, who are so easily impressed by size and ostentation.

Sometimes we see new things in truly unlooked-for places. One day I was standing by a hole in the ice on a small frozen river. Glancing underneath the ice, I saw an icicle hanging down toward the water. It was short and squat, but clear as glass, with a beautiful and perfect swirling shape. It had never occurred to me that there was anything at all on the bottom side of ice sheets. . . . Much of the holiness of winter (and of all the seasons) is in such hidden places, where God for a Creator's own delight has left a beauty seldom found by human eyes.

*If your life is so planned out you can't be flexible, you have forgotten how to be like a child.*

BARBARA JOHNSON

❄

DAVID RENSBERGER
*"The Holiness of Winter"*

## WHITE WORLD

I awoke to a world
of whitening wonder:
all the bareness of
winter landscape under
soft white snow
falling. . .
and still falling
as the dusk falls. . . .
The only color I can see:
a red bird in a whitened tree.
The only sound
   in a world gone still:
a towhee on my windowsill.

**RUTH BELL
GRAHAM**

*Clouds Are the
Dust of His Feet*

*Nothing speaks so much of*

*goodness as an apple*

*orchard in all its seasons.*

*There is beauty, even in*

*winter when only the bare*

*twigs and branches are seen.*

**FIONA
MACMATH**

*Spiritual Lessons
from an Apple
Orchard*

# The Road to the Cross

❄

*He knows our frame; He remembers that we are dust.*

PSALM 103:14

If the village house in Nazareth which they show tourists nowadays is anything like the one where the little boy Jesus lived, it was not much to speak of, by comparison with the ivory palaces He had left. He at whose word creation sprang into being was subject to the word of His mother Mary. He whose hands had made the worlds learned obedience in a dusty carpenter shop. When Joseph showed Him how to use a tool, did he hold the little hands in his and say, "Like this. Hold it this way"? The boy had to learn. He did not make tables and benches by divine fiat. He made them with tools held in human hands. He had to learn the skills, learn to be thorough, dependable, prompt, faithful. If He was ever tempted to cut corners, He did not yield to the temptation. . . . Surely He was gracious with the customers. He grew "in favor with God and man." The cheerful acceptance of humble work, the small testings of any boy's homelife were a part of His preparation for the great testings of His public years, a part of the road which led Him to the Cross.

*Keeping God on the throne of your heart is a daily discipline and delight.*

JAN CARLBERG

❄

## ELISABETH ELLIOT
*The Path of Loneliness*

*Week 10*

As I got out of the car one
evening, I happened to look
upward. For a moment,
I was transfixed. I had . . .
forgotten what the stars
looked like in winter. Bright
as ice and thick as snow—
drifts, they lay in heaps
across the sky. What I
had come to think of as
starry nights [in the city]
were nothing in comparison.

DAVID
RENSBERGER

"The Holiness
of Winter"

# A Sweet Fragrance

*Let us not grow weary while doing good,*
*for in due season we shall reap if we do not lose heart.*

GALATIANS 6:9

The ancient perfumers made use of the well-known power of oils and fats to absorb and give off odors. For example, olive oil formed the composition of the holy anointing oil used in the tabernacle, mentioned in Exodus 30:23–25. The oil base was then scented with liquid myrrh, fragrant cinnamon, cane, and sweet cassia. . . .

The perfumed incense made by the priests represented the loving self-sacrifice of God's people, as they brought themselves and their offerings to the altar.

Ecclesiastes tells us that a man's reputation is like the base ointment. It has the power to absorb and give off savors. This is common to men everywhere and not just to believers in Christ. God has given a reputation to every single human being living on the face of this earth. The ensuing savor or smell will depend very much upon the mixture of herbs that a man drops into the base oil of his character.

Did you know you can drop Christ, the finest, freshest, most fragrant herb of all into your character? And when Christ comes into your life, others will sense His presence by just being near you!

JILL BRISCOE
*How to Follow the Shepherd*

*As God works within us to make us holy, we become other-centered.*

CLAIRE CLONINGER

# The Centerpiece of Life

❋

*The Lord will deliver me from every evil work*
*and preserve me for His heavenly kingdom.*

2 TIMOTHY 4:18

A number of years ago my sister, Luci, gave me a volume I treasure . . . and in the front of the book she wrote these words from an old poem—words I immediately memorized and have never forgotten:

> Whom have we Lord, but Thee,
> Soul-thirst to satisfy?
> Exhaustless spring,
> The water is free,
> All other streams are dry.

We Christians, I have observed, frequently have trouble believing He is our only hope, security, light, and strength because we are so prone to try everything else. We automatically depend upon everything *except* the Lord. Yet still He waits there for us—patiently waiting to show Himself strong. . . .

He proves Himself strong in our weakness; He sheds light in our darkness; He becomes hope in our uncertainty and security in our confusion. He is the Centerpiece of our lives.

CHARLES SWINDOLL
*David: Man of Passion and Destiny*

## *Unfailing Love*

❄

*The LORD is great and greatly to be praised;*
*He is also to be feared above all gods.*

1   CHRONICLES   16 : 25

"Can anything make me stop loving you?" God asks. Watch me speak your language, sleep on your earth, and feel your hurts. Behold the maker of sight and sound as he sneezes, coughs, and blows his nose. You wonder if I understand how you feel? Look into the dancing eyes of the kid in Nazareth; that's God walking to school. Ponder the toddler at Mary's table; that's God spilling his milk.

"You wonder how long my love will last? Find your answer on a splintered cross, on a craggy hill. That's me you see up there, your maker, your God, nail–stabbed and bleeding. Covered in spit and sin–soaked. That's your sin I'm feeling. That's your death I'm dying. That's your resurrection I'm living. That's how much I love you."

*Outside of Christ there*
*is no law, no hope,*
*and no meaning.*

RAVI
ZACHARIAS

MAX   LUCADO
*In the Grip of Grace*

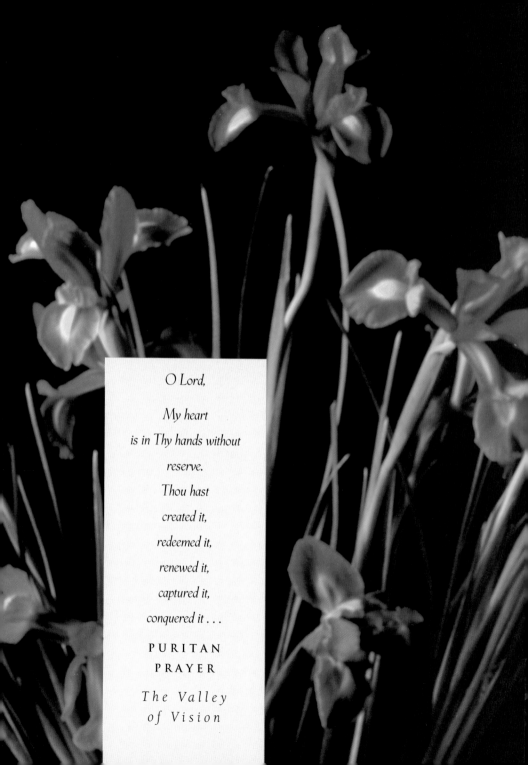

O Lord,

My heart
is in Thy hands without
reserve.
Thou hast
created it,
redeemed it,
renewed it,
captured it,
conquered it . . .

PURITAN
PRAYER

*The Valley
of Vision*

## God's Own Possession

---- ❄ ----

*Walk in love, as Christ also has loved us*
*and given Himself for us.*

EPHESIANS 5:2

Possessions of the powerful, wealthy or famous, no matter how common, can become extremely valuable, even priceless. Napoleon's tooth-brush sold for $21,000. Can you imagine—paying thousands of dollars for someone's cruddy old toothbrush? Hitler's car sold for over $150,000. Winston Churchhill's desk, a pipe owned by C. S. Lewis, sheet music handwritten by Beethoven, a house once owned by Ernest Hemmingway. At the Sotheby's auction of Jackie Kennedy Onassis's personal belongings, her fake pearls sold for $211,500 and JFK's wood golf clubs went for $772,500. Not because the items themselves are worthy but because they once belonged to someone significant.

Are you ready for a surprise? We fit that bill too. Think of the value of something owned by God. What incredible worth that bestows on us, what inexplicable dignity! We belong to Him. We are "a people for God's own possession" (1 Peter 2:9).

*No matter how little you have, you can always give some of it away.*

CATHERINE
MARSHALL

### CHARLES SWINDOLL
*Hope Again*

# Notes

❄

# A Job for God

※

*Blessed be the name of God forever and ever,*
*for wisdom and might are His.*

DANIEL 2:20

Goodness is a job for God. We must stop horning in on His business and instead ask Him to bring about our change: To those "who are far from righteousness," He says, "I am bringing my righteousness near" (Isaiah 46: 12–13).

Being godly does require discipline, but that discipline should never be construed as a rigorous technique. Following Christ requires effort, but it is the effort to stay close to Him and listen to His voice. Serious effort is needed if we are to focus on Him and become sensitive to His desires.

As we draw close to Him—walking with Him, talking to Him, listening to His words, relying on Him, asking for His help—His character begins to rub off on us. Quietly and unobtrusively His influence softens our wills, making us thirsty for righteousness, inclining us to do His pleasure, restraining our passions, keeping us from evil. . . . In His quiet love He takes all that's unworthy in us and gradually turns it into something worthwhile for Him.

*God's voice is often still and quiet and easily buried under an avalanche of clamor.*

CHARLES
STANLEY

※

DAVID ROPER
*Psalm 23*

*Every inch of the buttery is*

*crowded with goodness.*

*Even the windowsill in*

*winter is loaded in its*

*sunshine with a pot of chives,*

*a pot of parsley, and a rose*

*geranium whose leaves are*

*put into the bottom of the*

*cake tins to bake the*

*delicate flavor into the*

*best birthday cake of all.*

MARY MASON
CAMPBELL

*The New England*
*Butt'ry Shelf*
*Cookbook*

# Trust God Completely

❄

*Blessed are all who put their trust in Him.*

PSALM 2:12

Jesus did not say that we were not to be industrious, for birds are very industrious. They arise early in the morning and go out to collect the provisions that God has supplied. The flowers flourish and are beautifully clothed, but their roots reach down deep to tap the resources that God has put into the ground for their enrichment.

The birds remind us that food should not be our chief concern and the lilies show us that worrying over appearance does not make us beautiful. . . .

Two conflicting forces cannot exist in one human heart. When doubt reigns, faith cannot abide. Where hatred rules, love is crowded out. Where selfishness rules, there love cannot dwell. When worry is present, trust cannot crowd its way in.

The very best prescription for banishing worry is found in Psalm 37:5. "Commit thy way unto the Lord; trust also in him; and he shall bring it to pass." The word "commit" means to turn over to, to entrust completely.

*What we weave in time we must wear in eternity.*

BARBARA JOHNSON

❄

# Week 11

BILLY GRAHAM
*Unto the Hills*

Our own gardens are living
reminders that God is with
us, even in winter. The plants
and flowers may have lost
their leaves or blooms, but
deep inside
they are still nourished and
fed until spring arrives again.

**HARRIET
CROSBY**

*A Well-Watered
Garden*

# Living in Light of Eternity

❄

*The LORD will guide you continually
and satisfy your soul in drought.*

ISAIAH 58:11

Once when the Cleveland Symphony was performing *The Magic Flute* by Mozart, an electrical storm caused the lights to go out. Undaunted by the difficulties, the members of the orchestra knew the music so well that they completed the performance in the dark. At the end of the performance, the audience burst into thunderous applause, and a stagehand illuminated the orchestra and conductor with a flashlight so that they could take their bows.

It is much the same in the spiritual realm. If you know the Master, you can play His music even in the dark. You can live a holy life in an unholy realm. When caught between two worlds, the secret is to develop a mind-set that sees beyond the style of this world to the substance of the next.

*We can never know ourselves until we know Christ . . . whom to know is truth.*

RAVI
ZACHARIAS

❄

STACY AND PAULA RINEHART
*Living in Light of Eternity*

# Pay Attention to "Now"

---- ❄ ----

*He who has begun a good work in you will complete it*
*until the day of Jesus Christ.*

PHILIPPIANS 1:6

"I wish I were rid of diapers. Ugh! When this stage is over I'll be glad!"—"I wish I were rid of the preschool years. I'll be glad for a free number of hours!"—"I wish I were finished with teenagers. I can't wait till they all go off and I can start a new life!" . . .

Each stage goes so quickly, and life is soon gone. The danger of wasting the "now," because of sighing, quarreling, or being irritated into disregarding any of the positive things which will soon be gone, is a danger of being down at the bottom of the seesaw in an important balance. . . .

Life is not static. There are things to be discovered in each other, in our selves, in hidden talents and new interests, in freedom to do things which cannot be done now. The attention to be paid to the "now" should be balanced by the inner realization that there is a future with new things ahead. What is the "now" simply won't last, and the changes ahead should be like contemplating wrapped gifts with hidden contents!

EDITH SCHAEFFER
*What Is a Family?*

# Just Enough Light

❄

*You are my lamp, O LORD;*
*the LORD shall enlighten my darkness.*

2 SAMUEL 22:29

When I was just a lad, my dad and I used to go floundering, a popular pastime on the Gulf Coast. We'd carry a lantern in one hand and a two-pronged spear in the other (called a gig) as we walked along, knee-deep in the shallow water along the shore. As we walked, we'd swing the lantern back and forth as we searched the soft sand for the flounder that came up close to the shore in the evening to eat the shrimp and the mullet. The little lantern provided just enough light to reveal the fish down in the sand beneath the water . . . and just enough so that we could see a few feet ahead as we waded through the water. Actually, it was all the light we needed. It penetrated just enough of the darkness so that we could see where to walk, but not beyond that.

The same is true of the light we receive from God. At times we flounder along, trying to peer too far into the darkness ahead. Yet He gives us just enough light so that we can see to take the next step. That's all He gives and, in reality, that's all we need.

*Sorrow looks back,*
*worry looks around, and*
*faith looks up.*

BARBARA
JOHNSON

CHARLES SWINDOLL
*David: Man of Passion and Destiny*

Under the corner street-
lamps the [snow] flakes spun
and twinkled like fairies
trying their wings.
The whole earth wore
a jeweled wrap.

**MARJORIE
HOLMES**

*Love and Laughter*

# A Picture of Patience

❄

*We know that all things work together for good to those who love God, to those who are the called according to His purpose.*

ROMANS 8:28

The word "patience" as it is used in the New Testament, really has no true equivalent in the English language. Certainly it does not mean merely being placid and phlegmatic as so many people assume.

Patience is the powerful capacity of selfless love to suffer long under adversity. It is that noble ability to bear with either difficult people or adverse circumstances without breaking down....

Patience is the potent perseverance that produces positive results even under opposition and suffering. It is love, gracious, self-giving, pressing on, enduring hardship, because of the benefit it may bring to others....

*Discouragement may be awful, but it is not terminal.*

CHARLES
SWINDOLL

The patience of the New Testament writers is that of a small donkey bearing enormous burdens of firewood, sacks of grain or other produce for its owner. Year in, year out, surely, steadily, safely it transports loads of goods from place to place in quiet compliance with its master's wishes.

PHILLIP KELLER
*The Inspirational Writings of Phillip Keller*

# Notes

❄

# Windows of the Soul

❄

*By humility and the fear of the LORD are riches and honor and life.*

P R O V E R B S    2 2 : 4

G od stretched out the heavens, stippling the night with impressionistic stars. He set the sun to the rhythm of the day, the moon to the rhythm of the month, the seasons to the rhythm of the year. . . . He formed a likeness of Himself from a lump of clay and into it breathed life. He crafted a counterpart to complete the like‐ ness, joining the two halves and placing them center stage in His creation where there was a temptation and a fall, a great loss and a great hiding. God searched for the hiding couple, reaching to pick them up, dust them off, draw them near. . . .

*The values of heaven turn the values of earth upside-down.*

S U S A N   Y A T E S

We reach for God in many ways. Through our sculptures and our scriptures. Through our pictures and our prayers. Through our writing and our worship. And through them He reaches for us. . . .

His search begins with something said. Ours begins with something heard. His begins with something shown. Ours, with something seen. Our search for God and His search for us meet at windows in our everyday experience.

But we must learn to look with more than just our eyes and listen with more than just our ears, for the sounds are sometimes faint and the sights sometimes far away.

K E N   G I R E
*Windows of the Soul*

On a winter's day, nothing
reaches right to the bottom
of the soul like a good
homemade soup. . . . Just
add friends, light the fire,
and serve steaming.

TRICIA FOLEY

# Don't Lose Heart

❄

*We will walk in the name of the LORD our God forever and ever.*

MICAH 4:5

I once interviewed for what I considered my "dream job." The interview was intense and the process by which the employer reached a decision was long and drawn out. Then came the nerve–wracking wait to hear the results. Finally, I learned that another candidate had been chosen instead of me. I felt devastated for several days. My emotional turning point came when friends from out of town sent a gift of a beautiful blue hydrangea plant. A simple message was attached: "Don't lose heart!" I joyfully planted the hydrangea in a big redwood tub. With the support and love of friends such as these, I began to see that the job wasn't as important as I had imagined. My perspective and my feelings began to change.

> *What God wants is an obedient heart and availability.*
>
> CHARLES
> SWINDOLL
>
> ❄

Don't lose heart. Things change. God has made each of us able to change with the seasons—to rejoice during the good times and to weep during the bad times. The fellowship of God's people and the love of God will see us through.

# Week 12

HARRIET CROSBY
*A Well-Watered Garden*

The cattle and horses are
bedded warmly in the barn,
and the fireplace in the Old
Kitchen blazes with warmth
every evening at dusk. For
weeks the family
has gathered here for the
comfortable and satisfying
tasks of the late year.

MARY MASON
CAMPBELL

*The New England
Butt'ry Shelf
Cookbook*

# *Blue-Ribbon Love*

*Do not forget to do good and to share,
for with such sacrifices God is well pleased.*

HEBREWS 13:16

One day while driving down a country road, a woman named Ruth passed a small, wooden house with a sign outside that read "Quilts for Sale." She stopped, knocked on the door, and was greeted by [Martha], a little old woman in a faded gingham dress.

Martha led Ruth to a large cupboard and showed her beautiful quilts of every color and pattern imaginable. Pinned on each one was a blue ribbon.

"I make quilts, too," Ruth said, "but I've never been able to win a blue ribbon."

Martha replied, "My child, maybe your quilts don't have heart. Do you only want the blue ribbon? Every one of mine was made with someone special in mind."

We live in a day of shallow superlatives. Entertainers and athletes perform feats hailed "the greatest" by the world. But truly great human endeavors are those done for Jesus with some needy person in mind. And they bear the mark of eternal excellence.

*There is divine purpose in
bringing out the best
in one another.*

DENIS WAITLEY

DENNIS J. DEHAAN
*Our Daily Bread*

# God Is Cheering You On

*I will not leave you orphans: I will come to you.*

JOHN 14:18

God is for you. Your parents may have forgotten you, your teachers may have neglected you, your siblings may be ashamed of you; but within reach of your prayers is the maker of the oceans. God!

God is for you. Not "may be," not "has been," not "was," not "would be," but "God is!" He is for you. Today. At this hour. At this minute. As you read this sentence. No need to wait in line or come back tomorrow. He is with you. He could not be closer than he is at this second. His loyalty won't increase if you are better nor lessen if you are worse. He is for you.

God is for you. Turn to the sidelines; that's God cheering your run. Look past the finish line; that's God applauding your steps. Listen for him in the bleachers, shouting you name. Too tired to continue? He'll carry you. Too discouraged to fight? He's picking you up. God is for you.

MAX LUCADO
*In the Grip of Grace*

# Shut Those Doors Behind You

❄

*As you therefore have received Christ Jesus
the Lord, so walk in Him.*

COLOSSIANS 2:6

"**S**hut the door behind you!" my mother used to remind us as we all came banging in. . . . Shut it to cut out the draft, the cold—yes, that's generally what we mean. But in the larger sense, those words can be significant. For the habit of shutting doors behind us is invaluable to happiness; we must learn to shut life's doors to cut out the futile wind of past mistakes.

The man or woman you didn't marry. The house you didn't buy. The job you didn't take. That long-gone injury that is so much better forgotten. That loss, that devastating sorrow, that failure.

Forget it. Put it firmly away. To leave the door of memory even a little bit ajar is to provide passage for grief, remorse, regret—a flock of deadly enemies. . . .

Shut that door behind you. Lock it and throw away the key. The only doors that matter are those that we open today!

MARJORIE HOLMES
*Love and Laughter*

*We bring nothing
to God, and He gives
us everything.*

GARY THOMAS

Every afternoon Mama would
light a candle and put the
kettle on the hot plate. She
would arrange a small dish
of cookies, strudel, or banana
bread and stick a pansy or a
dandelion or a sprig of ivy in a
vase. She would get out her
teapot and teacups and open
her door a couple of feet—a
signal to the neighbors that it
was time to come and
"sip tea with Irene."

EMILIE BARNES

*If Teacups
Could Talk*

# Seek the Best

*The Lord is very compassionate and merciful.*

JAMES 5:11

The stone beside me marked the resting place of somebody's BELOVED WIFE who died in 1863 OF A FEVER. Beneath her name was a line of script, almost indistinguishable. I looked closer, wondering which biblical phrase her grieving children might have chosen. But it was not a quotation; it was a statement: EVER SHE SOUGHT THE BEST, EVER FOUND IT.

Eight words. I stood there with my fingers on the cool stone, feeling the present fade and the past stir behind the illusion we call time. A century ago this woman had been living through a hideous war. Perhaps it took her husband from her, perhaps her sons. When it ended her country was beaten, broken, impoverished. She must have known humiliation, tasted despair. Yet someone who knew her had written that she always looked for the best, and always found it. . . .

There was courage in the words, and dignity, and purpose. And a kind of triumph, too, as if they contained a secret of inestimable value. What you look for in life, they seemed to be saying, you will surely find. But the direction in which you look is up to you.

*God can take your trouble and change it into treasure.*

BARBARA
JOHNSON

ARTHUR GORDON
*A Touch of Wonder*

# Notes

❄

**O God,**
*The sea, dry land, winter cold, summer heat,
morning light, evening shade are full of thee,
and thou givest me them richly to enjoy.*

## PURITAN PRAYER
*The Valley of Vision*

# This "Waiting Stuff"

❄

*I will praise the name of God with a song,*
*and will magnify Him with thanksgiving.*

PSALM 69:30

Many times in my life God has asked me to wait when I wanted to move forward. He has kept me in the dark when I asked for light. To my pleas for guidance His answer has often been *Sit still, My daughter.* I like to see progress. I look for evidence that God is at least doing something. If the Shepherd leads us beside still waters when we were hoping for "white water" excitement, it is hard to believe anything really vital is taking place. God is silent. The house is silent. The phone doesn't ring. The mailbox is empty. . . .Of course for most of us this test of waiting does not take place in a silent and empty house, but in the course of regular work and appointments and taxpaying and grocery buying and trying to get the car fixed and the storm windows up; daily decisions have to go on being made, responsibilities fulfilled, families provided for, employers satisfied. How can we speak of waiting on God in the middle of all that? How be still?

There is a secret place where the Christian dwells. It is the shadow of the Almighty. Transactions take place there which none but God know.

*Worship lifts us*
*out of ourselves and reminds*
*us of who God is.*

SUSAN YATES

### ELISABETH ELLIOT
*The Path of Loneliness*

*What is more serene than the earth under a blanket of freshly fallen snow? Nature has come to a standstill. The only sound is ice crunching underfoot. People speak in muted tones. . . . This is a season of rest.*

WAYNE
JACOBSEN

*In My Father's
Vineyard*

## Dealing with Heart-Debts

*Forgive us our debts as we forgive our debtors.*

MATTHEW 6:12

D oesn't someone owe you something? An apology? A second chance? A fresh start? An explanation? A thank you? A childhood? A marriage? Stop and think about it . . . and you can make a list of a lot of folks who are in your debt. Your parents should have been more protective. Your children should have been more appreciative. Your spouse should be more sensitive. . . .

*If love is a feeling, we are all in trouble.*

CHARLES
STANLEY

What are you going to do with those in your debt? People in your past have dipped their hands in your purse and taken what was yours. What are you going to do? Few questions are more important. Dealing with debt is at the heart of your happiness. . . .

Jesus does not question the reality of your wounds. He does not doubt that you have been sinned against. The
# Week 13
issue is not the existence of pain, the issue is the treatment of pain. What are you going to do with your debts?

MAX LUCADO
*The Great House of God*

*Even on the coldest days,*
*I feel close to my garden*
*the minute I savor the*
*delicate flavors of my*
*favorite herbs and flowers*
*brewed in a cup*
*of traditional tea.*

EMELIE TOLLEY

# God Is the Destination

*Cast your burden on the LORD, and He shall sustain you;
He shall never permit the righteous to be moved.*

PSALM 55:22

Though we may feel as though we move through a labyrinth, we are being led by a power greater than ourselves. The solution to the original labyrinth was to walk through the maze using a string tied to the opening to avoid getting lost. In the Christian journey, the Holy Spirit is the string, guiding us through the confusing corridors of life.

Undergirding each of the choices we make in life, God is leading us. In our ignorance or in our false desires, we may make what we think is the "wrong" choice; however, because of God's redemption on the cross, there are no ultimate "wrong" choices. God redeems all our blunders, all our stupidity. The crucial choice is choosing God over not choosing God. Our job is to hold tight to the string. . . .

If God is the Destination of our spiritual journey, then we are freed from the fear of making bad choices. The present moment is all that matters. The future snuggles right into the present, and gives us peace.

*Trust with a childlike dependence on God, and no trouble can destroy you.*

BILLY GRAHAM

LESLIE WILLIAMS
*Night Wrestling*

# Listen Carefully

*I love those who love me,*
*and those who seek me diligently will find me.*

PROVERBS 8:17

This past year I drove from the Gulf Coast of Florida to the Atlantic Coast. My route took me along what is known as "Alligator Alley," an unswerving ribbon of asphalt that crosses the Everglades. Again and again, to break the monotony, I tried to tune in a good radio station, but the dial was almost entirely silent, with only two or three stations available. Because I was unable to pull in anything else, those few stations I received seemed to come through loud and clear. I found myself listening to programs I had not heard before simply because there was nothing else available. Then, as I neared the end of my journey and approached the city of Fort Lauderdale, the radio dial became so jammed with signals it was filled with static. . . . No one station stood out clearly. It was confusing. I would find a program I wanted to listen to, but in a few short miles it had been drowned out by other voices crowding in.

Our lives can be like that radio dial. We can be so jammed with signals coming from every direction that even when we tune in to the voice of God, He can get drowned out by other voices crowding in. If we are to hear Him clearly and loudly, there must be times of quietness built into our daily lives.

ANNE GRAHAM LOTZ
*The Vision of His Glory*

# Some Earthbound Wisdom

❄

*The eyes of the LORD are on the righteous,
and His ears are open to their cry.*

PSALM 34:15

When God says "no" it is not necessarily discipline or rejection. It may simply be redirection. You have pursued His will; you have wanted to do His will. You threw that piece of wood on the fire, and you saw your selfish desires go up in smoke. With all good intentions you said, "By God's grace I am going to pursue this." And here you are, thirty or forty years later, or maybe only five years later, and it hasn't worked out. . . .

*The spiritual life and the love of God are knit right into the texture of our lives.*

LESLIE WILLIAMS

The thing we have to do in our walk with God is to listen carefully from day to day. Not just go back to some decision and say, "That's it forever, regardless." We need to look at it each day, keep it fresh, keep the fire hot, keep it on the back burner, saying, "Lord, is this Your arrangement? Is this Your plan? If it is not, make me sensitive to it. Maybe You're redirecting my life."

God has all kinds of creative ways to use us—ways we can't even imagine and certainly can't see up there around the next bend in the road.

CHARLES SWINDOLL
*David: Man of Passion and Destiny*

# HOPE

*The long, gray winter*

*now is past—*

*the coldest we*

*have ever seen—*

*and I am glad*

*to note at last*

*earth's first bright*

*touch of green.*

RUTH BELL
GRAHAM

*Clouds Are the*
*Dust of His Feet*

# God Gives Perfect Gifts

❄

*The Father Himself loves you, because you have loved Me,*
*and have believed that I came forth from God.*

JOHN 16:27

I often see, shining in the deep blue of the sky just before dawn, the morning star. At twilight the sea sometimes reflects the pale rose and daffodil colors of the sunset. At night I awaken to find the room flooded with moonlight reflected from the sea, from the glass top of my desk by the window, and from the mirror of the dressing table. Flying at thirty thousand feet, I have seen glorious light shining on the towers and castles of thunderheads. What a gift are these lights of heaven! The same Father who gives them also gives us all other good and perfect things.

It is God's nature to give. He can no more "help" giving than He can "help" loving. We can absolutely count on it that He will give us everything in the world that is good for us, that is, everything that can possibly help us to be and do what He wants. How can He not do this?

*God's love for you*
*is unflappable; His*
*presence unstoppable.*

JAN CARLBERG

### ELISABETH ELLIOT
*Discipline: The Glad Surrender*

# Notes

*If Winter comes,*
*can Spring be far behind?*

PERCY B. SHELLEY

# Rest in God

✳

*Behold the eye of the LORD is on those who fear Him,
on those who hope in His mercy.*

PSALM 33:18

Few people know how to rest these days. Even on vacation, many people rush to cram in as much as they can before returning to their jobs, where they spend twice as much energy catching up on the work and mail that has piled up in their absence. Many of us need vacations just to rest from our vacations! Perhaps we have been looking for rest in the wrong places.

Jesus said, "Come unto me and I Will give you rest." Like peace, rest can be found only in one place, from one source, and that is the Lord Jesus Christ. . . .

Despite the headlines in the newspapers and some of the scenes we see on television, we know that all is going according to God's plan and foreknowledge.

Jesus gives us the ultimate rest, the confidence we need to escape the frustration and chaos of the world around us. Rest in Him and do not worry about what lies ahead. Jesus Christ has already taken care of tomorrow.

BILLY GRAHAM
*Unto the Hills*

*There is wonderful freedom and joy in recognizing that the fun is in the becoming.*

GLORIA GAITHER

# Acknowledgments

✳

*Grateful acknowledgment is made to the following
publishers and copyright holders for permission
to reprint copyrighted material:*

Jill Briscoe, *How to Follow the Shepherd* (Old Tappan, N. J.:
Fleming H. Revell, 1982).

Harriet Crosby, *A Well-Watered Garden* (Nashville: Thomas
Nelson, 1995).

Harriet Crosby, *A Place Called Home* (Nashville: Thomas
Nelson, 1997).

Elisabeth Elliot, *Love Has a Price Tag* (Ann Arbor, Mich.:
Servant Books, 1979). Servant Publications, Box 8617, Ann
Arbor, Michigan, 48107. Used with permission.

Elisabeth Elliot, *The Path of Loneliness* (Nashville: Thomas
Nelson, 1988).

Elisabeth Elliot, *Discipline, the Glad Surrender* (Old Tappan,
N.J.: Fleming H. Revell, 1982).

Jean Fleming, *Finding Focus in a Whirlwind World.* © Jean
Fleming, 1997.

Richard J. Foster, *Freedom of Simplicity* (San Francisco:
Harper & Row, 1981).

Ken Gire, *Windows of the Soul* (Grand Rapids: Zondervan,
1996). © Ken Gire, Jr., 1996. Used by permission of
Zondervan Publishing House.

Arthur Gordon, *A Touch of Wonder* (Old Tappan, N. J.,: Fleming H. Revell, 1974).

Ruth Bell Graham, *Clouds Are the Dust of His Feet* (Wheaton, Ill.: Crossway Books, 1992). © Ruth Bell Graham.

Billy Graham, *Unto the Hills* (Dallas: Word, 1996).

Billy Graham, *The Secret of Happiness* (Dallas: Word, 1985).

Liz Curtis Higgs, *Reflecting His Image* (Nashville: Thomas Nelson, 1996).

Marjorie Holmes, *Lord Let Me Love* (New York: Bantam Doubleday Dell, 1978).

Marjorie Holmes, *Love and Laughter* (New York: Bantam Doubleday Dell, 1967).

Phillip Keller, *The Inspirational Writings of Phillip Keller* (Dallas: Word, 1993).

Leonard E. LeSourd, ed., *The Best of Catherine Marshall* (Grand Rapids, Mich.: Chosen Books, 1993).

Terry Lindvall, *Surprised by Laughter* (Nashville: Thomas Nelson, 1996).

Anne Graham Lotz, *The Vision of His Glory* (Dallas: Word, 1996).

Anne Graham Lotz, *The Glorious Dawn of God's Story* (Dallas: Word, 1997).

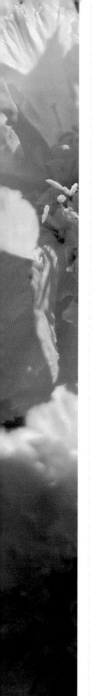

Max Lucado, *The Great House of God* (Dallas: Word, 1997).

Max Lucado, *In the Grip of Grace* (Dallas: Word, 1996).

Fiona MacMath, *Spiritual Lessons from an Apple Orchard* (Nashville: Thomas Nelson, 1996).

Catherine Marshall, *Adventures in Prayer* (Old Tappan, N.J.: Chosen Books, 1976).

Janette Oke, *The Father of Love* (Minneapolis: Bethany House Publishers, 1989).

*Our Daily Bread* (Grand Rapids: Discovery House Publishers, 1997). Used by permission of Discovery House Publishers, Box 3566, Grand Rapids, MI 49501. All rights reserved.

Gregory Post and Charles Turner, *The Feast: Reflections on the Bread of Life* (San Francisco: HarperSanFrancisco, 1992).

David Rensberger, "The Holiness of Winter," *Weavings; A Journal of the Christian Spiritual Life*, vol. 11, no. 6, November/December 1996. © 1996 by The Upper Room. Used by permission.

Stacy and Paula Rinehart, *Living in Light of Eternity* (Colorado Springs: NavPress, 1986).

David Roper, *Psalm 23: Hope and Rest from the Shepherd* (Grand Rapids: Discovery House, 1994). Used by permission of Discovery House Publishers, Box 3566, Grand Rapids, MI 49501. All rights reserved.

Edith Schaeffer, *Common Sense Christian Living* (Nashville, Tenn.: Thomas Nelson, 1983).

Edith Schaeffer, *What Is a Family?* (Grand Rapids, Mich.: Baker Book House, 1975).

Robert Schuller, *The Be Happy Attitudes* (Dallas: Word, 1985, 1996).

*Soul Searching: Meditations for Your Spiritual Journey* (Nashville: Thomas Nelson, 1995).

Charles Swindoll, *David: A Man of Passion and Destiny* (Dallas: Word, 1997).

Charles Swindoll, *Hope Again* (Dallas: Word, 1996).

Mother Teresa, *The Love of Christ* (San Francisco, Harper & Row, 1982).

Peter Wallace, *What the Psalmist Is Saying to You Today* (Nashville: Thomas Nelson, 1995).

Leslie Williams, *Night Wrestling* (Dallas: Word, 1997).

# Photo Credits

COVER
Rita Maas Photography


INTERIOR
Still Lifes: Joe Felzman Photography, Portland, Oregon.

Scenics: Steve Terrill Photography, Portland, Oregon.

Misc.: Tony Stone Images; pg. 36, 116.

Misc.: Superstock; pg. 122, 132.